THE GRATITUDE PATH

Other Books by Kent Millard
Lead Like Butler
The Passion-Driven Congregation
T.I.M.E.: Together In Ministry Everyday
Get Acquainted with Your Christian Faith
Spiritual Gifts

Kent Millard

THE
GRATITUDE
PATH

Leading Your Church
to Generosity

Abingdon Press
Nashville

THE GRATITUDE PATH:
LEADING YOUR CHURCH TO GENEROSITY

Copyright © 2015 by Abingdon Press

All rights reserved.

This book is printed on acid-free paper.

Library of Congress Cataloging-in-Publication Data

Millard, M. Kent, 1941-
    The gratitude path : leading your church to generosity / by Kent Millard.—First [edition].
        pages cm
    Includes bibliographical references.
    ISBN 978-1-63088-319-5 (binding: pbk.)
    1. Gratitude—Religious aspects—Christianity. 2. Generosity—Religious aspects—Christianity. 3. Christian giving. I. Title.
    BV4647.G8M55 2015
    254'.8—dc23

                                                                              2015010974

Scripture quotations unless noted otherwise are from the Common English Bible. Copyright © 2011 by the Common English Bible. All rights reserved. Used by permission. www.CommonEnglishBible.com.

Scripture quotations marked NRSV are from New Revised Standard Version of the Bible, copyright 1989, Division of Christian Education of the National Council of the Churches of Christ in the United States of America. Used by permission. All rights reserved.

Scripture quotations marked KJV are from The Authorized (King James) Version. Rights in the Authorized Version in the United Kingdom are vested in the Crown. Reproduced by permission of the Crown's patentee, Cambridge University Press.

15 16 17 18 19 20 21 22 23 24—10 9 8 7 6 5 4 3 2 1
MANUFACTURED IN THE UNITED STATES OF AMERICA

In memory of Bishop Rueben Job, who was my spiritual mentor, leadership coach, and model for living a grateful and generous life.

CONTENTS

INTRODUCTION

The Gratitude Path

Then Jesus took the bread. When he had given thanks, he distributed it to those who were sitting there. He did the same with the fish, each getting as much as they wanted.

—John 6:11

After taking a cup and giving thanks he said, "Take this and share it among yourselves."

—Luke 22:17

After taking the bread and giving thanks, he broke it and gave it to them.

—Luke 22:19

The Gratitude Path is the path in life that Jesus followed.

Five thousand people once came to hear Jesus preach, teach, and heal. When the evening came and the people were hungry, Jesus invited them to sit down and receive a meal. A young boy brought five loaves and two fish to Jesus. Jesus received the loaves and fish from the boy and gave thanks to God for them, and when they were distributed to the crowd, there was more than enough for all (John 6:1-11).

Later in his Gospel, John referred to the place where Jesus fed the five thousand as: "...the place where they had eaten the bread over which the Lord had given thanks" (John 6:23). The place where Jesus fed the five thousand is remembered by John as the place where "the Lord had given thanks"

(John 6:23). Before Jesus raised Lazarus from death to life he "looked up and said, 'Father, thank you for hearing me'" (John 11:41).

On the last night of his life, Jesus took a cup and a loaf of bread and gave thanks to God before he distributed them to his disciples.

In the Gospels, Jesus frequently gave thanks and praise to God. Jesus lived his life with an attitude of gratitude toward God in all the different circumstances of his life and called his followers to give constant thanks and praise to God as well.

When we follow Jesus along the gratitude path of life, we discover that we too live closer to God and experience God's abundance and blessings in our lives.

Unfortunately, rather than counting our blessings we are often people who ignore God's blessings in our lives and count our problems instead. Jesus did not spend his time counting his problems but rather trusting in God and giving thanks to God regardless of his circumstances. The Gratitude Path is the path Jesus followed in life and the path he invites us to travel with him.

This book is designed to help pastors and congregations focus on counting our many blessings and giving time, talent, and treasure to God out of gratitude for all God has first given to us. This is a stewardship resource based on the idea that we give to God not out of obligation, guilt, or a need to meet a church budget. Rather, we give thanks to God with a grateful heart because God has first blessed us in abundant ways.

After graduating from seminary with two advanced degrees, I went eagerly to my first appointment to serve God and the people of that parish. I knew a great deal about the Bible, church history, pastoral care, and theology. However, at my first church board meeting, I was not asked anything about the Bible, church history, pastoral care, or theology. I was asked what my plan was for the stewardship campaign in the fall.

Now, in my whole seminary education I had never had a course on stewardship campaigns or given a moment of thought about how to lead one. I told the board I would have to give their request some thought and would bring back a plan at the next meeting. The next day I visited a nearby experienced pastor and asked him what he did in a stewardship campaign. I copied everything he said and took it back to our board meeting, and we followed his stewardship campaign plan to the letter with good results.

I expect that my experience is not unusual. Few pastors have much experience in leading a local church stewardship campaign, and many pastors and laypeople are very uncomfortable in even talking about giving in a local church.

I have served as pastor in a two-point parish in a rural area, a suburban congregation, two downtown congregations, and a large regional church of over six thousand members. In every congregation the issue was the same: How do we best enroll people in giving time, talent, and treasure to support God's work through the congregation?

Since I retired from appointment to a local church, I serve as the volunteer Gratitude Coach for the eleven hundred United Methodist congregations in Indiana. This means I coach pastors and stewardship or finance committees in how to change the paradigm about giving to support God's work.

Frequently, I am invited to work with congregations who have financial challenges. I discover that many of them have no plan for giving and don't want anyone to talk about pledging or being generous in support of God's work. They simply receive an offering every Sunday and hope that it will be enough to cover their expenses. But as the congregation declines in membership, income goes down and they have to go to a part-time pastor and reduce their mission giving because they don't have the necessary resources.

I invite congregations not to start the conversation about giving with the needs of the congregation. I encourage them to start talking about the blessings God has already given each of us. I ask finance committee members to mention some of the ways God has blessed them with family, health, resources, and the ground we walk on and the air we breathe. I ask them to consider the blessing God gave all of us when God sent Jesus into the world to offer us unconditional love and forgiveness and to give us an eternally meaningful life now and forever.

When people begin to count their blessings, they realize that God has blessed us abundantly. And if we feel any sense of gratitude for these blessings, we want to give to God in appreciation for all God has first given us.

When a child receives a Christmas or birthday gift from someone, the parents will say to the child, "What do you say?" And the child will remember to say "thank you" to the person who gave the gift.

In a similar way we have all been given countless gifts from God and need to be reminded to say "Thank you, God" for all the gifts we have been given by our gracious God.

However, we are often reluctant to invite people to give generously to God out of gratitude. Consequently, giving in local Protestant congregations has declined as a percentage of income for many decades. The Empty Tomb is a stewardship research group located in Champaign, Illinois. The Empty Tomb research indicates that among church members of eleven Protestant denominations in the United States and Canada per-member giving as a percentage of income was lower in 2011 than in 1933 at the depth of the Great Depression. Per-member giving in 1933 was 3.3 percent of income while in 2011, after decades of unprecedented prosperity, giving to congregations had fallen to 2.3 percent of income.[1]

People often say that if we had more income we would give more to support God's work through the church. However, the truth is that it is not the amount of money in our wallets that determine our giving but the amount of gratitude in our hearts which determines how much we give to support God's work. I believe God has given the followers of Jesus a message that is essential for people to hear if they want to find meaning and purpose in life. I believe God has entrusted to us God's message of the unconditional love and forgiveness that comes to us in Jesus Christ. I believe there is a God-shaped hole in the soul of every person that can only be filled by God.

It breaks my heart to see churches declining when the people in their communities and people around the world need the life-giving message of Jesus that we are failing to deliver in life-giving ways.

My prayer is that this resource will bring life and joy back into congregations of all denominations all around the world by focusing on God's abundant blessings in our lives and our grateful response to those blessings.

I would encourage pastors and local church leaders to study this book, discuss the questions at the end of each chapter, and follow the guidelines for leading a Gratitude Campaign in your congregation. I believe that when we start counting our blessings rather than our problems it will lift the spirits of the people in the congregation and bring renewal and revitalization to all of the ministries of a local congregation.

When I was a district superintendent, a local congregation in my district needed a new pastor. The lay leader of the church told me that he wanted a "Bible-preaching pastor." We had a new seminary graduate who was a superb Bible student and thought he would be a good fit for this congregation.

However, about three months after the new pastor began serving at that congregation, I received a call from the lay leader. He was upset with the sermon the pastor had just preached. I asked what the sermon was about. He explained that their new pastor had preached about tithing and how important it was for faithful followers of Jesus to give 10 percent of their income to support God's work through the church.

I reminded him that he wanted a "Bible-preaching pastor" and that tithing was a part of the biblical message. He responded, "But I didn't want him to preach that part of the Bible!"

Many local church leaders do not want their pastor or anyone else to preach about giving our resources to God to support God's work. They may feel it is "unbiblical" to talk about giving in a congregation.

However, Jesus talked a great deal about our use of resources. Jesus knew that our refusal to give to God can be a huge block in our spiritual relationship with God. Here are just a few of the many passages where Jesus talked about the use of our resources.

Stop collecting treasures for your own benefit on earth, where moth and rust eat them and where thieves break in and steal them. Instead, collect treasures for yourselves in heaven....Where your treasure is, there your heart will be also. (Matt 6:19-21)

No one can serve two masters. Either you will hate the one and love the other, or you will be loyal to the one and have contempt for the other. You cannot serve God and wealth. (Matt 6:24)

All who want to come after me must say no to themselves, take up their cross, and follow me....Why would people gain the whole world but lose their lives? (Matt 16:24, 26)

When they came to Capernaum, the people who collected the half-shekel temple tax came to Peter and said, "Doesn't your teacher pay the temple tax?" "Yes," he said. (Matt 17:24-25)

"If you wish to be complete, go, sell what you own, and give the money to the poor. Then you will have treasure in heaven. And come follow me." But when the young man heard this, he went away saddened, because he had many possessions. (Matt 19:21-22)

I was hungry and you gave me food to eat. I was thirsty and you gave me a drink. I was a stranger and you welcomed me. I was naked and you gave me clothes to wear. I was sick and you took care of me. I was in prison and you visited me....I assure you that when you have done it for one of the least of these brothers and sisters of mine, you have done it for me. (Matt 25:35-36, 40)

Give, and it will be given to you. A good portion—packed down, firmly shaken, and overflowing—will fall into your lap. The portion you give will determine the portion you receive in return. (Luke 6:38)

When the day was almost over, the Twelve came to him and said, "Send the crowd away, so that they can go to the nearby villages and countryside and find lodging and food."...[Jesus] replied, "You give them something to eat." (Luke 9:12-13)

"Then he placed the wounded man on his own donkey, took him to an inn, and took care of him. The next day he took two full days' worth of wages and gave them to the innkeeper. He said, 'Take care of him, and when I return, I will pay you back for any additional costs.'...Which of these three was a neighbor to the man who encountered the thieves?" Then the legal expert said, "The one who demonstrated mercy toward him." Jesus told him, "Go and do likewise." (Luke 10:34-37)

Jesus said to them, "Watch out! Guard yourself against all kinds of greed. After all, one's life isn't determined by one's possessions, even when someone is very wealthy." (Luke 12:15)

The basic thrust of the teachings of Jesus was that God has given us all that we have and we are to use all that we have in ways that glorify God and serve others.

I served as lead pastor at St. Luke's United Methodist Church in Indianapolis for eighteen years, and during that time our giving to the annual budget tripled and people gave an additional $21 million for building expansion and missions.

The focus of our giving was on counting the blessings God has given us and giving back to God out of gratitude. We discovered that when we followed the Gratitude Path of thanking God for all our blessings, we arrived at the garden of abundance and there was always more than enough to support God's work through our congregation.

My prayer is that when congregations decide to conduct a Gratitude Campaign where people are invited to count their blessings and fill out a Gratitude Card to lay on the altar on Gratitude Sunday they will experience the joy of giving and the congregation will have more than enough to provide for the ministries of their church.

However, no stewardship campaign will be very effective in a congregation if there is not also vibrant worship; loving pastoral care; Bible study and prayer groups; fellowship opportunities; growth opportunities for children, youth, and adults; and effective mission outreach programs to the community. The Gratitude Campaign is most effective when the church is a place where people experience the living presence of God in worship and are growing in their faith through Bible study and mission outreach. Good stewardship in a congregation is not just a once-a-year program. Living with an attitude of gratitude toward God year round is the best way to make a once-a-year Gratitude Campaign most effective.

Chapters 1–5 provide the biblical and theological basis for a Gratitude Campaign with texts and sermon ideas for preaching on the Gratitude path of life. Chapter 6 is a detailed outline of how to conduct a Gratitude Campaign in your local congregation with a sample Gratitude Campaign sermon.

My prayer is that this resource will not only create more resources for ministry but also bring renewed spiritual vitality in the life of your congregation.

—Kent Millard
August 2015

"Just to Say Thanks"

One of them, when he saw that he had been healed, returned and praised God with a loud voice. He fell on his face at Jesus' feet and thanked him.

—Luke 17:15-16

Give thanks with a grateful heart.

—Henry Smith, "Give Thanks"

Count your many blessings, name them one by one, / And it will surprise you what the Lord has done.

—Johnson Oatman Jr.

"Just to Say Thanks"

When our son Kendall was in the fifth grade, our bishop appointed me to serve as a district superintendent. This meant that we would have to move to a new community.

My wife and I sat down with our two children and informed them that I had been appointed to a new position and we would have to move to another community.

Our son Kendall folded his arms and said, "I am not going to move. My best friend in the whole world lives here. I like my school, my church, and my room. For the first time in my life, I have a girlfriend. I am not moving."

We explained that we were a family and we would all have to move together even though it would be hard for all of us. "Besides," I said, "we are selling this house."

Kendall was adamant: "Then I will rent my room from whoever buys it!" He was determined not to leave his home and friends, but ultimately we all moved together as a family.

When we arrived at the district parsonage, Kendall and I went to a large family room downstairs. There in the middle of the room was a large table and on it was an electric train and track set up and plugged in. All we had to do was turn it on and the electric train started travelling around the tracks.

On the table was a large hand-printed sign that read: "For Kendall, from the Rueben Job family." Bishop Rueben Job was the former district superintendent who had just moved out of the district parsonage. Bishop Job knew how hard it was for Kendall to move to a new home, so his family decided to give their grown son's electric train to Kendall to ease his pain of moving to a new community.

Kendall was shocked. He said, "I don't even know these people. Why are they being so nice to me?"

Later that day a local United Methodist pastor and his son, John, who was the same age as Kendall, came over to help us unpack. Kendall and John became immediate friends and they spent the day playing with the electric train and exploring the neighborhood.

The next day, Kendall came into my home office with his hands cupped and filled with coins. He plopped the coins down on my desk and said, "Here, Dad, give this to God." I was surprised because Kendall had never done anything like that before.

I asked him why he wanted to give his money to God. Kendall shrugged and said, "Just to say thanks."

I asked, "Thanks for what?" He said, "You know—the train, John, and my new room."

Kendall had experienced some unexpected gifts and was filled with gratitude. He suspected God was responsible for giving him these wonderful gifts, so he wanted to say thanks to God by giving some of his money to God.

I thanked him for expressing his gratitude to God with a generous gift to God. Then I asked him, "How did you decide how much you were going to give to God to say thanks?"

Kendall said he opened his bank and counted out all his money on his bed and then decided to give God half of it. I didn't tell him you only have to give 10 percent!

Our son realized that he had been given some unexpected generous gifts from God and he wanted to express his gratitude to God by giving some of his money to God, "just to say thanks."

The real motivation for giving some of our time, talent, and treasure to God is ultimately just to say thanks for all the gifts God has already given to us.

When we think about it, everything we are and have is a gift to us from the hands of our generous God.

We did not create the marvelous and miraculous body in which we live. Our bodies were created by God through our parents and given to us for our journey here on earth. We did not create the spark of God's spirit that God placed in each of us we call our soul or the image of God within us. Our eternal soul is a gift from God.

We did not create our spouses, partners, children, parents, grandchildren, or friends. All the people we care for were created by God and given to us.

We did not create the ground we walk on; the air we breathe; the sun that gives us life; the birds, flowers, and animals; the food we eat; and everything that enables us to live on this earth. Everything in creation is a gift from the hands of our generous God.

We did not create Jesus Christ who came and lived among us to teach us how to trust God totally, surrender ourselves into God's loving hands, and discover an eternally meaningful life through his life, death, and resurrection.

The truth about life is that everything we are and everything we have is a loving gift from the hands of a kind and generous God.

We give some of our time, talent, and treasure back to God not out of obligation, guilt, or a need to meet a church budget. We give to God "just to say thanks" for all that God has first created and given to us.

Gratitude to God is the fundamental scriptural reason and our motivation for giving our time in worship, our talent in service, and our financial gifts to support God's ministry in the world.

From Stewardship Campaigns to Gratitude Campaigns

When we give out of gratitude we transform the annual local church stewardship campaign into a Gratitude Campaign. When gratitude becomes the focus of our campaign we change the pledge card or estimate of giving card into a Gratitude Card, and we transform Stewardship or Consecration Sunday into Gratitude Sunday. A stewardship campaign is usually based on the idea that God is the creator of all we are and have, and we are therefore obligated to be good stewards of God's creation. A Gratitude Campaign recognizes that all we are and have is a gift from God, but we give back to God out of gratitude not obligation.

Stewardship campaigns are often based on Jesus's parable about the landlord who went away leaving his servants in charge of his property. In Matthew 25:14-30 Jesus told a parable about a landlord who gave three of his servants different amounts of money (talents) to manage while he was gone. When the landlord returned, he rewarded or punished each servant according to how they used or failed to use the money he had given them. It is true that we are all given differing amounts of resources in this life and are ultimately accountable to God for how we use or misuse them.

However, the primary image of our relationship to God in the New Testament is not that we are hired servants responsible to an absent landlord but that we are children of a loving heavenly Father who is never absent but is always present with us.

In the parable of the prodigal son (Luke 15:11-32), when the wayward son "came to his senses" he decided to return to his father to beg for a job as a servant on the family farm. However, when the loving father saw his disobedient son returning home, he was "moved with compassion...[he] ran to him, hugged him, and kissed him." The father put a robe on his son's shoulders, a ring on his finger, and sandals on his feet as a sign that his son was welcomed home as his beloved son, not simply as a servant. Because of the father's unexpected loving actions, the parable is sometimes called the Parable of the Loving Father.

According to Jesus, our basic relationship to God is as beloved sons and daughters of God. Our function as God's beloved children is to be the faithful and loving servants of God. According to the Parable of the Loving Father, we are primarily beloved children who are always part of the family rather than simply hired servants.

Throughout the Gospels, Jesus taught his followers to call God Father, not to indicate that God was male, but to indicate that God was a loving and compassionate parent to God's earthly children.

In fact, the Aramaic word Jesus used for God is the word *Abba* which means "Father." When Jesus prayed to God in the Garden of Gethsemane before his arrest he prayed: "Abba, Father, for you all things are possible.

Take this cup of suffering away from me. However—not what I want but what you want" (Mark 14:36). Paul also used Jesus's word *Abba* to refer to God when he wrote: "You received a Spirit that shows you are adopted as his children. With this Spirit we cry 'Abba, Father'" (Rom 8:15). In Galatians 4:6 Paul also wrote: "Because you are sons and daughters, God sent the Spirit of his Son into our hearts, crying 'Abba, Father.'" Undoubtedly, Jesus called God *Abba* himself and Paul carried on Jesus's tradition in some of his letters to the followers of Jesus.

The Aramaic word *Abba* is the word a young Jewish child would call his or her father. To call a father "Abba" indicates a very personal and intimate relationship—like a young child would have with a loving father. It would be like a child calling his or her father "Daddy" or "Papa" today.

The biblical scholar Marcus Borg writes: "Why would a first-century Jewish person address God as "Papa" when his tradition typically used much more formal terms of address for God?...It also seems likely that this intimate term of address for God expressed the intimacy of Jesus' own experience of God."[1] When the disciples asked Jesus to teach them to pray, Jesus said, "Pray like this: Our Father who is in heaven..." (Matt 6:8-9). In fact, in Matthew 6:1-34 Jesus refers to God twelve times as "your father" or "your heavenly Father." Jesus wanted us to know God as he knew God, which is as loving "Abba"—a caring Father, which makes us all children of a loving God.

The primary image Jesus used for his relationship to God and for his followers' relationship to God is that of a loving Abba who cares deeply for all people.

Jesus also affirmed that all we are and have ultimately belongs to God, and we are temporary stewards of these gifts. Therefore, we are called to be good stewards of God's gifts while we have possession of them on earth. But our primary relationship to God is not that of hired servants of an absent landlord but as grateful children of a loving and ever-present Abba.

We are good stewards of all God has given us not out of fear of punishment but out of deep love and gratitude for all of the gifts of life our heavenly Abba has first given to us.

Give Thanks with a Grateful Heart

Musician Don Moen has recorded a beautiful contemporary chorus that expresses our gratitude to God for all God has already done for us.

Give thanks with a grateful heart,
give thanks to the Holy One[2]

When followers of Jesus count all of the blessings God has already given to us, we want to "Give thanks with a grateful heart."

We give thanks that God gave us Jesus Christ to teach us what God is like, to demonstrate complete trust in God, to live a life of unconditional love, and to give his life on a cross and rise again for our salvation. When we realize the depth of God's everlasting love for us, our hearts are filled with thanksgiving and gratitude.

We give thanks not only for the gift of Jesus Christ but for everything God has given to us and done for us. When we think of everything God has already done for us, we want to give thanks with a grateful heart.

The only question is whether or not we have a "grateful heart."

Jesus said, "What fills the heart comes out of the mouth. Good people bring out good things from their good treasure" (Matt 12:34-35).

Our problem is that sometimes we have cold and hard hearts rather than grateful hearts.

When we go see a medical doctor for an examination, the doctor frequently begins the examination by putting a stethoscope to our chest and listens to our hearts. By listening to our heartbeat the doctor can determine a great deal about the health of our heart and indeed our whole body.

In a similar way, we need to examine our hearts frequently to determine if we are living with a "grateful heart" for all God has given us. However, sometimes we discover that we are not living with a "grateful heart" but with a "hard, judgmental, and condemning heart," which makes us unhealthy in body, mind, and soul.

A question we should ask ourselves frequently is: "Am I living with a grateful heart or an ungrateful, hard heart?"

In 1965 I participated in Dr. Martin Luther King Jr.'s voting rights march in Selma, Alabama. On one occasion we marched to the courthouse in Selma and an African American person was denied the right to register and vote. We stood on the steps of the courthouse while angry people shouted ugly words at us. An African American pastor prayed for those shouting at us "that God would turn their hearts of hate to hearts of love." Forty years later, I spoke to a group of Alabama pastors and told them about my experience in Selma in 1965. Afterwards, one pastor came up to me and said: "I was in Selma at the same time you were, but I was on the other side. I did awful things to people then."

"What changed you?" I asked.

He said, "Jesus Christ. I got so filled with hatred I couldn't stand myself. My wife invited me to a Methodist revival meeting, and I went forward, knelt at the altar, confessed my sins, and Christ came into my heart and replaced my hatred and bitterness with love. I decided to become a United Methodist minister to share God's unconditional love for all people."

Then I remembered the prayer of an African American pastor forty years earlier: "Turn their hearts of hate to hearts of love," and realized his prayer request had been fulfilled in the life of this pastor.

The Good News is that Christ can turn all of our hearts from hearts filled with hate, anger, negativity, jealousy, resentment, or bitterness into hearts filled with love, compassion, faith, and gratitude. A Gratitude Campaign always begins with a heart filled with love and gratitude for God.

Count Your Blessings

"Count your blessings, name them one by one, / count your blessings, see what God has done."

An older hymn also reminds us to focus on the blessings God has given us. In 1897, Johnson Oatman Jr., a local Methodist pastor and businessman, wrote "Count Your Blessings" which has enabled millions to focus on their blessings from God so God can help them overcome the challenges in their lives.

> When upon life's billows you are tempest tossed,
> When you are discouraged, thinking all is lost,
> Count your many blessings, name them one by one,
> And it will surprise you what the Lord has done.
>
> Count your blessings, name them one by one,
> Count your blessings, see what God has done!
> Count your blessings, name them one by one,
> And it will surprise you what the Lord has done.

Johnson Oatman reminds us in the midst of the challenging times in our lives "when we are discouraged thinking all is lost" it is then that we most need to "count our many blessings." When we are overwhelmed with problems we need to refocus ourselves and count the blessings God has given us to regain hope and the ability to live victoriously in the midst of the challenges of life.

What we count, we increase. When we spend our time counting all of our problems, it seems as though we always have more problems to count. We all know people who are filled with complaints about their lives, the lives of those around them, and all the conditions of the world. When we ask people who focus their attention on their problems how they are, they always have more complaints to share with us.

Conversely, when we ask people who focus their attention on the blessings in their lives how they are, they always seem to have more blessings to share. The Gratitude path leads to generosity in our congregations when we count our many blessings and give time, talent, and treasure back to God, just to say thanks.

Where Are the Other Nine?

On one occasion, Jesus and his disciples went through a Samaritan village on their way from Galilee to Jerusalem. As they approached the village, ten lepers called out, saying, "Jesus, Master, show us mercy!" (Luke 17:13).

Leprosy is a painful disfiguring disease that often eats at our fingers, toes, ears, and nose. When a person was discovered to have leprosy in the time of Jesus, they were cast out of the village where they lived. They could no longer live with their families in their own homes, work at their jobs, or attend the synagogue or the market. Instead, they had to live outside the village away from everyone else. They survived by begging food from all those who entered or left their village. They also had to stay a stone's throw away from those who travelled along the road to insure that others would not be infected by their disease.

Luke tells us that the ten lepers "[kept] their distance" when they shouted out, "Jesus, Master, have mercy on us!" (vv. 12-13).

I suspect most people just ignored these ten lepers and pretended that they didn't see or hear them as they travelled along the road to the village. But Jesus "saw" them (v. 14). He paused and looked intently and compassionately at them and heard their request for healing.

Jesus then told them, "Go, show yourselves to the priests" (v. 14). The priests in the village would have to examine the lepers to determine if, in fact, they had been healed and could return to their normal lives.

Luke tells us that "as they left, they were cleansed" (v. 14). As they obeyed the command of Jesus and started toward the town, they suddenly discovered they were healed. They took a step of faith and while obeying Jesus's instruction, discovered they were healed. Perhaps when we follow Christ's instructions immediately as they did, it is then we are healed and made whole in our lives.

Can you imagine the joy these lepers experienced when they felt their faces, looked at their hands and feet, and discovered they were healed? Now how did they respond to this gift of healing?

Nine of them continued running into the village to show themselves to their loved ones and the priest so they could return to their normal lives. They were thankful for the healing but forgot to say thanks to the healer.

But one of the nine, when he discovered that he was healed, turned around and ran to Jesus. Luke says, "One of them, when he saw that he had been healed, returned and praised God with a loud voice. He fell on his face at Jesus' feet and thanked him" (vv. 15-16).

This man was a Samaritan, a member of a religious group that the Jewish people of Jesus's day looked down upon. But he was the only one of the ten healed lepers to return to Jesus, fall on his knees, praise God with a loud voice, and thank Jesus for making him whole and restoring his life.

This healed Samaritan is the model for what Christ calls us all to do. We are all called to become aware of the ways God has blessed us and come to Christ, fall on our knees, and offer our heartfelt prayers of thanksgiving for all the blessings God has given us.

Jesus responded by asking, "Weren't ten cleansed? Where are the other nine?" (v. 17).

Where *were* the other nine healed men? I suspect they continued running into the city. They were eager to show themselves to the priest, to be certified as healed so they could return to live with their families and resume their previous lives. They must have been overjoyed with this healing but they neglected to thank the healer. They received the blessing but failed to thank the one who gave the blessing.

Sometimes we are like the nine who failed to return to give thanks to God. We have all been blessed by God with the gift of life itself and the love that makes life meaningful. We enjoy the gifts of God but often fail to return to God to say thanks for all these gifts.

Thank God for What God Has Already Done for Us

I did not grow up attending church because, for the first ten years of my life, my dad was a practicing alcoholic. I was born in Hereford, Texas, and during my early years, our family moved around a great deal because my dad would go on a drinking binge, miss work for a week, and get fired, forcing us to move to another town for another job. I also remember many quarrels between my parents over my dad's drinking.

Eventually we moved to Faith, South Dakota, a small town in western South Dakota with a population of five hundred people. My mother ran a café and my dad drank up the profits.

There was only one bar in Faith at the time, a municipal bar owned by the city. The bartender was the only employee, and he was also the sheriff. He would sell alcohol to someone until they got drunk and then arrest them for public intoxication. He would put them in the jail that was attached to the bar and they would have to pay a fine to get out of jail. It was the town's fund-raising system.

My dad was caught in that system. He would get drunk and then thrown in jail, and the next day my mother would send me to the jail with the bail money. Dad would always be ashamed of himself for getting drunk and thrown in jail and would promise to never let it happen again. But a week or two later we went through the same story all over again.

One night the bartender/sheriff decided not to put my dad in jail but to take him to a meeting where three men were meeting in a new group called Alcoholics Anonymous. These men took my dad under their wing. They took him to a ranch about twenty miles from town to dry out and learn the steps of AA.

Dad says that he was walking across the prairie one day trying to memorize the steps of Alcoholics Anonymous. The first couple of AA steps are to admit that we are powerless over alcohol but that there is a power that can save us from this addiction.

Dad said to himself, "I am powerless over alcohol. I have stopped drinking a thousand times but I always go back to drinking."

Dad continued. "Believe there is a power that can save us from this addiction." Dad thought to himself, *I wish that was true.*

Then he felt it. He felt as though he was surrounded by a bright light and a living presence. He fell to his knees and cried out, "God, if you are real, save me because I can't save myself."

In that moment of total surrender, Dad felt the presence of God come into his life and give him a peace he had never known before. When he got up from the prairie, he knew he would never drink again.

When Dad returned to town and told us he would never drink again, it came from his deep spiritual experience and he never took another drink of alcohol for the rest of his life.

Then Dad said, "Now we need to go to church." I was ten years old and had never attended worship. I didn't know why people went to church. I asked, "Why do we have to go to church now?" Dad explained, "We need to go to church to thank God for getting me sober."

I was very thankful that my dad became sober, but it never occurred to me that therefore we should go to church to thank God for making it happen.

So we started attending a small Methodist church in our town. When we attended worship services, we sang songs of praise and thanksgiving to God. It occurred to me that people sing songs of thanksgiving to God in churches because of what God has already done in their lives. I was thankful to God for what God had done for my dad and our family and thought that God must have done something for all the other people in the church since they came every Sunday and sang songs of praise to God.

I thought people came to church to thank God for what God has already done in their lives, and when I got to seminary years later, I discovered this was a very good theology.

One Sunday our family joined the church where the pastor was a woman. The first Methodist minister I ever met was a woman and she was extremely loving and accepting of all people. The pastor invited our family to come forward to take the vows of membership. After we affirmed our faith, she had us face the congregation. Then she invited everyone in the congregation (all twenty-five people) to come forward and welcome us unto this family of faith.

I remember standing at the front of the church when people came up and hugged me and welcomed me into the congregation. I cried. It felt so good to be welcomed by this loving group of people. They all knew that my dad had been an alcoholic and was often put in jail, but it didn't make any difference to them. They opened their arms and welcomed us warmly. They practiced the motto of the United Methodist Church years before it became official: "We are a church with open hearts, open minds, and open doors."

I didn't know much about God or Jesus, but I loved church people because they are the people who welcomed and loved an alcoholic and his family. I think I fell in love with the church that day.

When I reflect on it, I realize that we go to church today for the same reason we first went to church years ago: to thank God for all that God has already done in our lives.

The reason we all come to worship on Sunday mornings is just to say thanks for all the gifts of life we have already received. We come to worship to offer our songs of praise and prayers of thanksgiving for all God has already done for us. We put our monetary offerings in the offering plates and lay them on the altar as a way of saying "thanks" to our loving heavenly Father for all the blessings God has given to us as children of God.

A Gratitude Campaign in a local congregation is a time to refocus our attention on all the ways God has blessed us and remind us to give our time in worship, our talent in service, and our treasure to support God's work through the church. Our motivation for giving is not out of obligation or guilt or to meet a church budget. Our motivation for giving is "just to say thanks" for all God has first given us.

When we give to God "just to say thanks," we are starting down the Gratitude Path that leads us to joyful generosity.

Questions for Discussion

1. Do I attend worship "just to say thanks" for all God has already given me?

2. Am I living with a grateful heart or a hard heart?

3. Am I more likely to count my blessings or my problems?

4. Am I more like the nine lepers who accepted the healing but forgot to thank the healer or like the one leper who returned to give thanks to God?

CHAPTER TWO

GIVE THANKS IN EVERY SITUATION

Rejoice always. Pray continually. Give thanks in every situation because this is God's will for you in Christ Jesus.
—1 Thessalonians 5:16-18

If the only prayer you said in your whole life was "Thank You" that would be enough.
—Meister Eckhart

Thou hast given so much to me, give me one thing more—A Grateful Heart.
—George Herbert

Give Thanks in Every Situation

After forty-eight years of marriage, my wife, Minnietta, passed away from pancreatic cancer. The entire family, including our two children, their spouses, our seven grandchildren, our friends, and our congregation, was devastated by Minnietta's death.

Anyone who has ever experienced the tragic loss of a dearly loved family member knows the pain and emptiness one feels when a loved one is no longer physically present. It often feels as though a part of yourself is gone and there is a deep loneliness and longing for the one who has passed away.

After Minnietta died, I was resentful about losing her. I kept thinking that it shouldn't have happened. She exercised, ate well, and meditated regularly. We had plans to celebrate our fiftieth wedding anniversary with a cruise. But she died and all our plans changed.

One day while I was writing in my journal about my resentment, this phrase came to mind: "accept what you cannot change." I realized that no matter how much I resent it I can't change the fact that Minnietta died. It was as if God was telling me to accept what I could not change. The feeling was so powerful that I remember saying out loud, "I accept her death." It was hard to say but when I said it and meant it, a peace came over me that I had not known in months.

One day during my devotions, I read Paul's words to the followers of Jesus in Thessalonica: "Rejoice always. Pray continually. Give thanks in every situation because for this is God's will for you in Christ Jesus" (1 Thess 5:16-18).

I recognized that Paul did not say give thanks *for* every situation but *in* the midst of every situation we may face. I was not thankful that I lost my wife, but I realized that there was so much to be thankful for in the midst of her loss.

In my journal I wrote down all of the things I was thankful for in the midst of her death.

I was thankful for her deep faith. Her theme during the last year of her life was "Trust God no matter what." She constantly reminded me and everyone who came to see her that she had always trusted God with her life and the lives of those she loved so she would place her complete trust in God whether she lived or died.

She loved the song with these words: "When we are living we are in Christ Jesus / and when we're dying it is in the Lord. / Both in our living and in our dying / we belong to God, we belong to God."[1]

This is a musical rendition of Paul's words to the followers of Jesus in Philippi: "Christ's greatness will be seen in my body, now as always whether I live or die. Because for to me, living serves Christ and dying is even better" (Phil 1:20-21).

Both in our living and in our dying we belong to God.

I thank God for her deep faith and total trust in the God who created, loved, and sustained her all her life here on earth. Today whenever I am faced with a challenge, I remember her faith and say to myself, "Trust God no matter what."

I am also thankful that God created her in the first place and gave her to me as my wife. I thank God for the artistic gifts and spiritual wisdom she possessed. I thank God she was such a loving mother and devoted grandmother. I thank God for her ability to lead others to experience the living presence of God in their lives.

Sometimes people would ask me if I ever ask why she died. I respond by telling them the only "why" question I ask is, "Why was I so blessed to have her for my wife for forty-eight years?" After all, she could have had a husband who was tall, dark, and handsome with hair and she got stuck with me!

I am thankful God gave her to me as a loving life partner, best friend, spiritual mentor, and guide.

I am also thankful for the gift of eternal life. I know that this is not the end of her journey. Death is simply a doorway through which we all must pass as we continue our journey with God. My image is that we were all with God in eternity and then we came to the earth and were enfleshed in a human body. We will live in this body for a long time or a short time and then we will leave the body behind and return home to God.

French philosopher, scientist, and Jesuit priest Pierre Teilhard deChardin once wrote these words: "We are not human beings having a spiritual experience, we are spiritual beings having a human experience."[2] I thank God for the gift of being a part of her spirit's human experience in this world.

In the midst of loss, I thank God for being part of a loving faith community that surrounded Minnietta with prayers, love, and support during her illness and held our family in their hearts as we walked through this "valley of the shadow of death" (Ps 23:4 KJV).

In the midst of our loss, I discovered I could follow Paul's spiritual guidance when he wrote, "Give thanks in *every* situation because this is God's will for you in Christ Jesus" (1 Thess 5:18, emphasis added).

It is easy to give thanks to God when everything is going well. When our families are happy and healthy, when we enjoy our work and our congregations are growing in faith and outreach, it is not hard to give thanks to God.

However, the real test of the depth of our faith is whether or not we can give thanks to God even in the midst of challenges, tragedies, suffering, and death. In the midst of the most painful loss I have ever experienced, I can testify that there is always something for which we can give thanks to God.

Today, when we encounter someone facing a challenge in their lives, we listen deeply and compassionately and then we might ask, "What is there in this situation for which you can give thanks to God?"

People often ask, "What is God's will for my life?" or "What does God want me to do?" We often ask this question in terms of what job or profession might God call us to do.

However, Paul gives us an answer to this question in terms of the attitude we should take regardless of our work or situation. Paul tells us that the will of God is the same for everyone and that is to always give thanks to God in every situation we face in life.

"Give thanks in every situation because this is *God's will* for you in Christ Jesus."

If someone asks us what the will of God for them might be in any situation, we can always reply by saying: "The will of God for you right now is to find something in your present situation for which you can give thanks to God."

The truth is that when we find that for which we can be thankful in every situation, then our spirits are lifted, we count our blessings, and we move away from the "woe is me" approach to living with an attitude of gratitude.

Many people in our congregations and communities live with cynical, angry, bitter, and depressing attitudes toward life.

A Gratitude Campaign in a local congregation will not only generate generous giving but it will also lift the spirits of people and change the cultural mood from fear to faith, hate to hope, and pessimism to peace.

Now Thank We All Our God

A favorite Christian hymn for expressing our gratitude to God is the seventeenth-century hymn by a German Lutheran pastor named Martin Rinkart entitled "Now Thank We All Our God." Many congregations sing this hymn on the Sunday before Thanksgiving as a way of expressing our gratitude to God for all the gifts of life.

However, most people do not know that this hymn was written by Pastor Rinkart during a time of great suffering.

Pastor Rinkart was pastor to a Lutheran congregation in the walled city of Eilenburg, Germany, during the Thirty Years' War. Eilenburg was a city of refuge for political and military fugitives, which meant it became severely overcrowded and experienced deadly pestilence, poverty, and famine. Armies overran it three times. Even though Pastor Rinkart had barely enough to provide for his own family, he opened his home to provide food and shelter to countless people in need. In 1637 the people of Eilenburg experienced a severe plague and as the only surviving pastor in the city Pastor Rinkart conducted as many as fifty funerals a day for those who died during the plague. Pastor Rinkart's wife also died of the plague and he conducted her funeral.

One might think that a pastor who had experienced so much pain, suffering, and death might be upset with God or have a negative view of life.

However, in the midst of a plague that killed thousands of people including his own beloved wife, Pastor Rinkart wrote a powerful hymn of gratitude and thanksgiving to God. Imagine a pastor who had experienced such great suffering writing these words of thanks to God:

> Now thank we all our God, with heart and hands and voices,
> Who wondrous things has done, in whom this world rejoices;
> Who from our mothers' arms has blessed us on our way
> With countless gifts of love and still is ours today.
>
> O may this bounteous God through all our life be near us,
> With ever joyful hearts and blessed peace to cheer us;
> And keep us still in grace, and guide us when perplexed;
> And free us from all ills, in this world and the next.[3]

Pastor Rinkart modeled Paul's admonition to "Give thanks in every situation." In the very midst of great suffering and death he still gave thanks to God. Frequently, when people of deep faith go through great suffering and loss they come to a spiritual place of total trust and thanksgiving to God that has little to do with the actual conditions of suffering they are experiencing. They come to the place of thanking God for God's sake and not because they have been given a life free of suffering.

In spite of being surrounded by death, Pastor Rinkart affirmed that our bounteous God is always near us, keeps us in grace, guides us when perplexed, and frees us from all ills in this world and the next.

Paul had also gone through a time of great suffering when he wrote "give thanks in every situation."

When Paul first visited Thessalonica and preached the good news of the life and teachings, death and resurrection of Jesus, he aroused great opposition. Consequently, Paul's opponents drove him out of the city and hounded him on his missionary journey to other communities. During his missionary journeys Paul was beaten by the Roman soldiers with thirty-nine lashes three different times, imprisoned several times, stoned and left for dead outside a city wall, shipwrecked, and nearly starved to death.

When Paul and Silas were in Philippi, they were arrested by the authorities and given a severe flogging with rods and thrown into jail with their feet fastened in the stocks. In spite of their suffering and pain, Paul and Silas sang songs of praise and thanksgiving to God. There was an earthquake that opened the doors of the prison. This led the jailer to free Paul and Silas, and the jailer and his family became followers of Christ (Acts 16:22-34).

Perhaps one of the goals of the Christian life is to come to the point in our faith where we can give our thanks and praise to God in every situation and in spite of the pain and suffering we might be going through.

My image is that when we offer prayers of thanksgiving to God and sing songs of praise to God in the midst of suffering, the very act of praising God lifts us up out of the pit of suffering and into the loving, healing presence of God. As long as we wallow in the pit of suffering and complain about our lot in life, we are stuck in despair. If we want to help people experience joy and hope in the midst of the challenges of life, we need to lead them in offering prayers of thanksgiving and singing songs of praise to God in every situation.

Unconditional Gratitude

Jesus modeled the unconditional love of God for all humanity when he gave himself on the cross for the sins of all people. Paul expresses it with these words in his letter to the Romans: "But God shows his love for us, because while we still were sinners Christ died for us" (Rom 5:8).

God's love does not depend on our goodness or on deserving it but on the nature of God's unconditional love for us as God's precious children.

Our response to God's unconditional love is our unconditional gratitude.

However, often our gratitude to God is conditional. Our gratitude is frequently conditioned on how well things are going in our lives. When things are going well in our families, our businesses, our personal relationships, our congregation, and our communities, we are eager to give our thanks and praise to God.

But when the storms and challenges of life come, we often sink into despair and discouragement and see little reason to give our thanks and praise to God. Our praise to God is conditioned on what we perceive to be our blessings from God.

Paul teaches us to practice unconditional gratitude, to give thanks to God in every situation of life.

The truth is that everyone will go through discouraging times in life. We may lose a loved one or a job or our health or a marriage or a relationship. When this happens, it is easy for us to become discouraged, disappointed, and depressed. When things go wrong in our lives, it is easy to become negative and cynical and want to give up.

However, in the face of disappointment in life a person can choose to become bitter or to become better.

The world is full of bitter and cynical people for whom life has not turned out the way they wanted. Life has not lived up to their expectations and they are upset, angry, and pessimistic.

Yet there are others who have lived through exactly the same disappointing experiences in life and have used them as an opportunity for personal growth and to develop deeper compassion for all people.

When I look back on my life I realize that the difficult times in life have been a great source of personal spiritual growth.

On one occasion, I was the lead pastor in a congregation where there was a significant amount of interpersonal conflict among staff members. I was sure I could manage it, but the more I sought to be a manager and mediator the worse the conflict became. I was very discouraged in myself and my leadership.

During that time, my morning devotional passage one morning was John 15:1-11, where Jesus compares himself to a grapevine, his Father to the vine grower, and his followers to the branches that are to produce the fruit.

In this passage Jesus says that the branches that bear no fruit are cut off and thrown away. And those branches that are fruitful are pruned or trimmed back so they might bear more fruit: "He [God] removes any of my branches that don't produce fruit, and he trims any branch that produces fruit so that it will produce even more fruit" (John 15:2).

We had a congregation growing in membership and attendance that was very fruitful in deepening faith and expanding compassion to others. It suddenly occurred to me that I was being trimmed or pruned so that we might become even more fruitful.

I received my humbling, frustrating experience as a leader as a pruning from God, but it was done so that we might become more fruitful as a congregation. For me this frustrating experience was used by God to humble me and make me more fruitful in reaching new people with the good news of Jesus Christ.

Frustrating experiences and disappointments can either make us bitter or make us better depending on how we choose to respond to them. When we give thanks in all situations we rise up and become better people and more faithful servants of Christ.

A Most Grateful Person

The most grateful person I have ever known was a parishioner named Lou Loocke. She was eighty-five years old when I first met her and she was able to give thanks to God in every situation. At the time, I was a pastor in South Dakota, where the winter weather is frequently cold with deep snow.

On Sunday mornings when it was cold and snowy, most people came to worship grumpy about the snow storm. But not Lou. When Lou came to church on a snowy Sunday morning, she would always say, "Isn't the snow beautiful! Did you see how the evergreen trees are so lovely when they are covered with such beautiful white snow? Look at the snowdrifts! The wind and snow make wonderful artistic shapes for us to enjoy. Aren't we blessed to live in an area where we get to enjoy the beauty of the snow?"

In the summer time, when it was terribly hot, Lou would come into church and say, "I just love the sunshine. The sun makes the flowers and grass grow and gives us life. I thank God for the sunshine."

On one occasion, Lou fell and broke her hip. When I came into her hospital room to visit her, Lou said, "Kent, thank you so much for coming to see me." I asked her how she was doing and she replied, "I am so blessed to be in this hospital room."

I asked, "Why are you so blessed to be in this hospital?" Lou said, "They bring you food three times a day and you don't have to fix it! There are wonderful doctors and nurses who come to see you several times a day and they are so concerned and loving. Friends come to see you and pray for you. I have received all of these wonderful get-well cards from so many loving people. And, not only that, but now I have time to read all of these devotional books that I have collected over the years. I feel so blessed to have this time in the hospital."

I asked her how her hip was and she said, "Oh, it's fine. I am just so blessed to be here for a while."

I have discovered that Lou's attitude of gratitude is different than most people I visit when they are in the hospital. While many of us constantly focus on the problems and challenges of our lives, Lou focused on the blessings she could see in even the most challenging times of her life.

Someone once said that Lou must have had a very easy life because she was always giving thanks to God in every situation.

I explained that the opposite was the case. Lou had had a very difficult life. When she was a young woman she and her husband had five young children. Then, when her husband was in his midthirties, he suddenly died of a heart attack and left Lou to be a single mother with few resources to raise her children. Lou worked as a waitress, cleaned houses, and took in laundry to make ends meet and provide for her five young children. She worked very hard and successfully raised and gave a college education to her five children.

Later in life she remarried and a few years later her second husband took his own life in a time of despair. So she went through deep pain and suffering with the loss of her second husband. Lou had lived through some very difficult times in life, but she was able to give thanks to God in every situation and in spite of all the challenges she faced.

I asked Lou how she remained so positive and thankful in the midst of all the challenges of her life. Lou said, "I say this prayer of surrender every morning: 'Father, in your hands and keeping now I place all my affairs; all my many situations, all my hopes, all my cares. All my loved ones fully knowing they can neither fail nor fall when they follow your direction for your love surrounds us all.'"

Lou explained to me that when we can surrender control of our lives and the lives of those we love into the loving hands of God, we can live each day simply counting our blessings and giving thanks in the midst of all the challenges of our lives.

When we count our blessings in every situation of life and give thanks with a grateful heart, we discover how to live the life Christ called us to live when he said, "I have said these things to you so that my joy will be in you and your joy will be complete" (John 15:11).

The followers of Jesus seek to give thanks in all circumstances and in every situation as we walk the Gratitude Path hand in hand with our loving God.

Questions for Discussion

1. How do you give thanks to God in every situation?

2. Have you ever had a "pruning" experience in your life? How did you respond?

3. How do you surrender all of your concerns into the hands of God and trust God no matter what?

GIVE AND IT WILL BE GIVEN TO YOU

Give, and it will be given to you. A good portion—packed down, firmly shaken, and overflowing— will fall into your lap. The portion you give will determine the portion you will receive in return.

—Luke 6:38

What I mean is this: the one who sows a small number of seeds will also reap a small crop, and the one who sows a generous amount of seeds will also reap a generous crop.

—2 Corinthians 9:6

Bring the whole tenth-part to the storage house so that there might be food in my house. Please test me in this, says the LORD of heavenly forces. See whether I do not open all the windows of the heavens for you and empty out a blessing until there is enough.

—Malachi 3:10

You can't outgive God.

—Rev. Grace Huck

Bring the Full Tithe?

When I was in high school and heard a pastor preach about tithing or giving 10 percent of my income to God each week, I felt that was totally unrealistic. I had a job in my dad's gas station and wanted to save my money to go to college, so I was not at all interested in giving 10 percent of my meager income away. I would put a dollar or two in the offering plate on Sundays and I thought I was being generous enough.

When I graduated from college and got married, my wife was committed to giving a tithe of her income from summer jobs and part-time college jobs to support God's work through the church. So we had a difference of opinion over how much we should give to God.

We went to seminary together and both of us had small part-time positions in local churches. We had so little income we could not afford a car or to go out to eat in a restaurant. We barely had enough money to pay for our tuition, books, and room and board at the seminary.

However, my wife insisted that we give a tithe of the income from our part-time jobs to God. She quoted to me the words from the prophet Malachi in the Old Testament: "Bring the whole tenth-part to the store house so that there might be food in my house. Please test me in this, says the Lord of heavenly forces. See whether I do not open all the windows of the heavens for you and empty out a blessing until there is enough." (Mal 3:10).

She believed that if we were faithful to God in our tithing, God would take care of us and "open all the windows of the heavens... and empty out a blessing until there is enough."

I gave her my arguments against tithing.

I told her that Malachi is in the Old Testament and we don't follow much of the Old Testament literally, like sacrificing bulls on the altar. We are New Testament Christians and follow the commandments of Christ who was criticized for breaking Old Testament laws like healing on the Sabbath. I told her Jesus doesn't specifically command us to tithe, so it is not one of the primary commands we need to follow. I argued that if we just obey Jesus's Great Commandment to love God with our whole being and our neighbor as ourselves that would be enough.

Besides, I explained, we are barely able to pay our rent and buy food, so surely God wouldn't expect us to go hungry so we could give a tithe to the church.

Then I gave her my best argument of all. I explained that I was studying to be a minister and would be giving 100 percent of my time and energy in the service of God so we shouldn't be expected to give 10 percent of our income as well.

But she was persistent in her faith and commitment to tithing, so we gave 10 percent of our small income to God each week in spite of my resistance.

I was sure that when we tithed we would not have enough money for food and necessities, but an amazing thing happened. We didn't suffer at all. Somehow there was always enough income for our necessities even though we were giving 10 percent to God each week.

Then I think a miracle happened. Just before Christmas, we received a letter and check in the mail from a man in our home state. He explained that he was a farmer and each fall after he harvested his crops he gave 10 percent of his income to God. Part of that 10 percent he would give to a seminary student. He didn't know us well, but he picked our name out of a list of seminary students from our Annual Conference and decided to send us a special gift.

He had enclosed a check for five hundred dollars, which would be like giving a gift of twenty-five hundred dollars today. We were overcome with joy and wept because of his generous gift. We walked around our small one-room apartment saying over and over, "I can't believe it." Then we got down on our knees and thanked God for this totally unexpected and generous gift. Out of a deep feeling of gratitude for his generosity and commitment to tithe we gave 10 percent of this gift to support God's work through the churches where we worked.

We wrote and called to thank this generous farmer for tithing his income and for sharing part of his tithe with us. We made arrangements to see him personally when we returned to our home state to share how much his generous gift meant in providing for our needs and to our growth in faith.

Then I remembered Malachi's words: "Bring the whole tenth-part . . . see whether I do not open all the windows of the heavens for you and empty out a blessing until there is enough." We experienced an overflowing blessing and gave thanks to God for it.

Now, our motive for tithing our income to God is not so that we will automatically get more blessings in return. If we tithe to God in order to get more blessings from God in return, our motive for tithing is selfish and self-seeking.

The Christ-centered motive for tithing is simply to express our heartfelt gratitude to God for all God has first given us. Tithing challenges us not to focus on ourselves and our own needs but to focus on God and how everything we are and have is a gift from the hands of a generous God.

God has given us 100 percent of all we have and allows us to use up to 90 percent of our resources to provide for our basic human needs, meet the needs of others, and bring glory to God. When we give 10 percent back to God, it is simply a practical way to say thank you for the 100 percent God has first given us.

During one local church Gratitude Campaign, I brought ten apples to the front of the congregation and laid them on a table. I explained that these ten apples represented everything God has given us. They represent all the people we love; all that we possess; our own bodies, minds, and souls; the homes we live in; the food we eat; the ground we walk on; the air we breathe; and the sun that gives us life. These apples represent everything we are and have and they are a gift from the hands of our generous God.

God has given us all ten apples and asks us to just give one apple back to God to say thanks for all God has first given us and to support God's work in the world. I picked up one of the apples and said this apple represents our tithe as we give one-tenth of all God has given us back to God to say thanks for all the other gifts from God.

Then I took a knife and cut off part of the tithe apple I was going to give to God. I explained that I had some unexpected bills and I had to use part of the tithe apple to pay these bills. Then I cut off some more of the tithe apple and explained that we needed a new car so I had to use part of the tithe apple to pay for it. I cut off more of the tithe apple and explained that we wanted to take a big family vacation and we needed to use some of our tithe apple to help pay for that family vacation.

Ultimately, I just had the core of the tithe apple left in my hand. I went over and put it in the offering plate on the altar and said, "God has given us all we are and have but often we use it for ourselves so we only have an apple core left to express our gratitude to God." This dramatic illustration helps us recognize that everything is a gift from God and to consider our generosity or lack of generosity in expressing gratitude for God's gifts to us.

A tithe is not a legalistic requirement like paying dues to belong to a service club or social organization. We give at least 10 percent of our income to support God's work to express our gratitude for all God has first given to us. Some followers of Jesus give at least 10 percent to support God's work through their local church while others give 10 percent or more both to support God's work in the local church and to support God's work in ministries beyond the local congregation. Some followers of Jesus feel that all of their giving to God's work in the world should be included in their tithe. Other followers of Jesus may begin by giving 2 percent or 3 percent of their income to God with the intention of increasing their percentage of giving each year until they are "giving the full tithe."

God is aware of our motives for giving and only desires that gratitude becomes our basic motivation for giving our time, talent, and treasure to God. If we tithe to God and then boast about our generosity, God is aware of our egotistical attitude and weeps over our self-centeredness. When we give out of gratitude, we also give up our need to control how the gifts are used or the need to be recognized for our generosity. Jesus said, "Happy are people who are humble" (Matt 5:5), and when we want recognition for our gifts, our pride, not our humility, is revealed.

Jesus also emphasized humility in giving when he said, "But when you give to the poor, don't let your left hand know what your right hand is doing so that you may give to the poor in secret. Your Father who sees what you do in secret will reward you" (Matt 6:3-4).

When our hearts are filled with a deep sense of gratitude to our compassionate God, we give eagerly, abundantly, and extravagantly to support God's work throughout the world without wanting to control how the gifts are used or getting recognition for our gifts.

Jesus never commanded his disciples to give 10 percent of their income to God. Jesus wanted us to give 100 percent of ourselves to God so that everything we are and have is devoted to the loving service of God and others. When we surrender ourselves totally and completely into the hands of God, we seek to use 100 percent of our time, talent, and treasure in ways that bring honor and glory to God and serve the needs of others.

Give and It Will Be Given to You

Jesus made a similar point about being blessed through our giving in the Gospel of Luke.

Matthew collected many of the teachings of Jesus and put them in what we call the "Sermon on the Mount" in Matthew 5–7.

Luke collected many similar teachings of Jesus and put them in what we call the "Sermon on the Plain" in Luke 6:17-49:

> Jesus came down from the mountain with them and stood on a large area of level ground. A great company of his disciples and a huge crowd of people…joined him there.…Jesus raised his eyes to his disciples and said…"give, and it will be given to you. A good portion—packed down, firmly shaken, and overflowing—will fall into your lap. The portion you give will determine the portion you receive in return." (vv. 17-38, selected verses)

Jesus used the image of a bag being filled with grain. When a person went to the market to buy grain to make bread, they would take a cloth bag to be filled. Grain would be poured into the bag until it seemed full, but the person buying the grain would shake it and press the grain down in order to get as much grain as possible in the bag.

Jesus used the image that when we open up our hearts and lives and give time, talent, and treasure to God, God responds by filling our lives full to overflowing with love, blessings, joy, and peace.

The truth about life is that when we open our hands and give generously to God, then we are in the open-handed position to receive blessings from God. Conversely, if we live with our fists tightly closed keeping our resources only for ourselves, we close ourselves off from receiving the blessings God wants to put in our hands.

It is with open hands that we give to God and it is with open hands that we receive from God. We need to open our hands and give to God so we have open hands to receive from God.

Life is a circle of receiving and giving. We receive gifts from God, we give them back to God and others, then we receive gifts again and we give again. Life is cyclical. If we receive gifts from God and keep them only for ourselves, we die spiritually. It is only when we receive and give, receive and give that the cycle of life brings meaning and joy to us.

An analogy of this process is the circulation of blood in our bodies. Our hearts receive blood from the other parts of the body and then it pumps the blood back to the other parts of the body. Our hearts are continually receiving and giving, receiving and giving.

If our hearts received the blood from other parts of the body and said, "I will keep all the blood for myself" we would die. Our hearts are intended to receive blood and give blood back to the body, and if our hearts stopped this flow of receiving and giving we would die.

In a similar way, God pours blessings into all of our lives. But sometimes we become egotistical and self-centered and want to keep all the blessings from God for ourselves. When we hold on tightly to all the gifts God gave us to share with others, we shrink into little selfish, unfulfilled people.

"Give, and it will be given to you."

On another occasion, two brothers came to Jesus because they were fighting over the division of a family inheritance. Jesus realized that the fundamental problem for both of them was their greed for more.

Jesus said to them both, "Watch out! Guard yourself against all kinds of greed. After all, one's life isn't determined by one's possessions, even when someone is very wealthy" (Luke 12:15).

Jesus knows about our tendency to be greedy and want to hold on to our resources and possessions rather than sharing them with God and others.

The antidote for the disease of greed is generosity. One cannot be greedy and generous at the same time.

If the green monster of greed has taken possession of us, the best way to defeat that monster is to become generous and give something away. In this case we give not because God or someone else needs it but we give because we need to be healed and freed from the life-destroying illness of greed.

"Give, and it will be given to you."

Paul made a similar point in his second letter to the Christians in Corinth. In the first century there was a famine in Jerusalem and many followers of Jesus were in dire need for food. Paul notified all of his churches about this need and made arrangements to travel to each of them to receive gifts for the needs of their fellow Christians in Jerusalem.

Paul wrote to the Corinthians to tell them he would come to see them and collect their offering and take it to Jerusalem. In the process of encouraging them to be generous in this special offering for the poor, he revealed his theological understanding of giving.

Paul wrote, "What I mean is this: the one who sows a small number of seeds will also reap a small crop, and the one who sows a generous amount of seeds will also reap a generous crop" (2 Cor 9:6).

In an agricultural society, Paul used an analogy of sowing seeds and reaping a harvest. Everyone who read Paul's letter would understand his point. If you only planted a few barley seeds (sow sparingly) in the spring, you would only have a small crop of barley to harvest in the fall (reap sparingly).

And if you planted a large number of seeds (sow bountifully), then you would harvest a more bountiful crop of barley in the fall.

The point for the Corinthians was obvious. If they only gave a small amount for the offering for the poor in Jerusalem, they would experience a small amount of joy and satisfaction from their gift. But if they gave a generous and bountiful amount, they would reap a bountiful harvest of joy and satisfaction in their lives.

Jesus and Paul both teach us that when we give generously we receive bountifully and when we refuse to give generously according to our means, we receive little fulfillment or satisfaction in our lives.

In one of the congregations I served a man came up to speak to me during our annual Gratitude Campaign. I had talked about giving sparingly and reaping sparingly or sowing bountifully and reaping bountifully.

The man was a successful businessman. He explained that he had never been a very generous giver to the church. He had an abundance of resources but he said he could never imagine himself giving a large gift to the church. However, he said he was going to make a very significant commitment to support God's work through the church just to see if he would grow spiritually through his generous gift. I took his hand and offered a prayer thanking God for his generosity and for all the ways God had blessed him in the past and would bless him in the future.

About six months later, that same businessman came to talk with me again.

He said, "I don't understand this. I am no better at running my business this year than I was last year, but this year my business has really taken off. My income has increased significantly and I can give even more than I thought I could to support God's work through the church. You don't think this had anything to do with my making a generous commitment to support God's work do you?"

I replied that we do not give to God in order to get more back from God. But when we are generous it somehow opens us up to the possibilities of receiving greater blessings from God and life. I told him that he is experiencing what Jesus meant when he said, "Give, and it will be given to you" and what Paul meant when he wrote, "[if you sow] a generous amount of seeds [you] will also reap a generous crop."

I explained that this is a spiritual growth matter and not an economic investment matter. We don't invest in God's work so that we will get a better return on our investment. If that is our attitude, we are simply feeding our greed, focusing on ourselves, and giving to God so that we will ultimately get more in return.

We give to God according to our means out of a heart filled with gratitude and thanksgiving for all God has first given to us. God looks in our hearts and sees our motive and when God recognizes we are motivated by gratitude and humility over all the blessings God has given us, then the result is frequently abundant blessings.

"Give, and it will be given to you."

A pastor once prayed this prayer before the offering was received in the worship service: "O God, make our gifts according to our blessings, lest thou make our blessings according to our gifts. Amen."

This pastor realized that some people are greatly blessed with time, talent, and treasure but their gifts to the God who blessed them are meager. Conversely, many people who have very few resources in this world are often very generous in their giving. The facts are that lower-income people typically give a larger percentage of their income to support God's work than people with greater resources.

Jesus stated it so clearly when he said, "Give, and it will be given to you. A good portion—packed down, firmly shaken, overflowing—will fall into your lap. The portion you give will determine the portion you receive in return." (Luke 6:38).

Gratefulness Leads to Great Fullness

When we live a life of gratefulness for all the blessings God has given us, we experience great fullness in our lives.

Dr. Robert Emmons is a psychology professor at the University of California in Davis, California. Dr. Emmons specializes in the psychology of gratitude. He has studied extensively on the positive effects of expressing gratitude on a regular basis on our health in body, mind, and soul.

Dr. Emmons conducted a study in which he asked one group of student volunteers to keep a gratitude journal for two months. At the end of each day they agreed to write down in a journal all of the things for which they were grateful.

Another randomly chosen group of students were asked to keep a complaint journal for two months. They were asked to write down at the end of each day all of their complaints or all of the negative things that had happened to them during that day.

At the end of the two months, Dr. Emmons personally interviewed all of the students in both groups. Dr. Emmons summarized his findings in an article on Gratitude and Well-Being with these observations:

> Those who kept gratitude journals on a weekly basis exercised more regularly, reported fewer physical symptoms, felt better about their lives as a whole, and were more optimistic about the upcoming week compared to those who recorded hassles or neutral life events....Participants who kept gratitude lists were more likely to have made progress toward important personal goals (academic, interpersonal, and health based) over a two-month period compared the subjects in the other experimental conditions.[1]

Both groups were randomly selected. The only difference was that one group focused on expressing their gratitude for their blessings in life and the other group focused on their complaints about life. The ones who kept a gratitude journal experienced more fulfillment in life than those who simply counted all their complaints about life.

The truth is that when one lives a life of gratefulness, one has great fullness and fulfillment in life. Gratefulness leads to great fullness.

When the offering is brought forward in worship in many congregations, the Doxology is sung:

> Praise God, from whom all blessings flow;
> Praise him [God], all creatures here below;
> Praise him [God] above, ye heavenly host;
> Praise Father, Son, and Holy Ghost. Amen.[2]

Whenever we sing the Doxology, we are recognizing that it is God "from whom all blessings flow." Therefore we give some of our blessings back to God out of gratitude for all the blessings God has first caused to flow into our lives.

God has so constructed life that when we open up and give generously of our time, talent, and treasure to God, we are in a position to receive blessings from the hand of our generous God.

"Give, and it will be given to you."

Questions for Discussion

1. What do you believe about tithing or giving a certain percentage of your income to God out of gratitude for all God has first given you?

2. What experiences do you have in receiving unexpected blessings in your life?

3. Have you ever kept a gratitude journal? What was your experience like?

CHAPTER FOUR

GOD LOVES A CHEERFUL GIVER

*Everyone should give whatever they have decided in their heart.
They shouldn't give with hesitation or because of pressure. God
loves a cheerful giver.*

—2 Corinthians 9:7

*I have said these things to you so that my joy will be in you and
your joy will be complete.*

—John 15:11

*This is the day the LORD acted;
we will rejoice and celebrate in it!*

—Psalm 118:24

I've got joy like a fountain in my soul.

—Spiritual

During one of our Gratitude Campaigns, I preached under the title "God Loves a Cheerful Giver."

My point was that the way we can give cheerfully and joyfully to God is if we give out of a heart filled with gratitude for all God has first given us.

Sometimes we don't give cheerfully. Sometimes we give grudgingly out of obligation. Since we made a commitment to support the church with our "prayers, presence, gifts, service, and witness" we are therefore obligated to give to support the work of the church. We look at our giving to the church in the same way we look at our obligation to pay our dues to other organizations to which we belong. But when we give out of obligation to pay our dues or fair share, we are not giving cheerfully to God out of gratitude but giving out of the pressure of obligation.

Sometimes we may give out of guilt. We see pictures of starving children around the world and we feel guilty because we have more than enough to eat. So we may give to support God's work out of a feeling of guilt because we have so much and they have so little. But when we give out of guilt we are not giving cheerfully to God out of gratitude.

Sometimes we may give simply to support the church budget. The finance committee may explain to the congregation that expenses are going up in the church and that we have prepared a budget with a 2, 3, or 4 percent increase for the next year. Therefore everyone needs to increase their giving by at least 2, 3, or 4 percent so that we can pay the bills and keep the church open for another year. I have even heard church leaders say, "If you want the church to be open for your funeral, then you need to give to keep the doors open." But when we give "just to keep the church doors open" we are not giving cheerfully with a glad and generous heart.

When we encourage people to give on the basis of obligation, guilt, or a need to meet the church budget, we are focusing on the church and its needs rather than on God and God's generous gifts to us.

We need to change the focus. Our focus should be on God and the way God has already blessed us full to overflowing. When we count our many blessings from God, our hearts are filled with gratitude and we want to give cheerfully and joyfully.

Once I may have taken this idea of cheerful giving too far in my congregation. In my message I suggested that if you can't give cheerfully and joyfully out of gratitude for all God has first given you, perhaps you shouldn't give at all. Perhaps you need to wait until your heart is right. Perhaps you shouldn't give anything until you have come to the place where you have a heart filled with gratitude and joy over all that God has first given you. Then you are ready to be a cheerful giver.

After that message I discovered that the chair of our finance committee was not happy with my message. He explained that he agreed we should give cheerfully and out of a heart filled with gratitude but that "we will take it from a grouchy person as well."

As local church finance leaders, it is our responsibility to change the focus from the needs of the church to our blessings from God and we will discover people will give cheerfully and joyfully out of gratitude for all God has first given us.

In 2 Corinthians 9, Paul encourages the Christians in Corinth to give generously to support people in need in Jerusalem during a time of famine and starvation. The need is real but Paul doesn't want people to give out of obligation or guilt.

It is in this context that Paul writes: "Everyone should give whatever they have decided in their heart. They shouldn't give with hesitation or because of pressure. God loves a cheerful giver. God has the power to provide you with more than enough of every kind of grace. That way, you will have everything you need always and in everything to provide more than enough for every kind of good work" (vv. 7-8).

Paul specifically tells us not to give "with hesitation or because of pressure." Therefore, we don't give out of obligation or guilt.

Instead, Paul focuses our attention on God's abundant blessings in our lives. "God has the power to provide you with more than enough." Again, change the focus from the needs of the church to the abundant blessings God has already poured into our lives.

Paul concludes that when we focus on God's abundant blessings, we realize we already have "everything you need always" so we can "provide more than enough for every kind of good work."

Paul told the followers of Jesus in Corinth that God had already provided them with everything they needed to live a full life. I think Paul would say the same thing to most of us; God has already provided us with everything we need to live a full life. Paul doesn't say that God has provided us with everything we *want* but with everything we *need*.

There are two problems with focusing our attention on getting everything we want. The first problem is that we might not get all we want and become frustrated and upset. The second problem is that we might get everything we want and still be unfulfilled and without meaning in our lives. Therefore, our focus should be on thanking God for the abundance of blessings we have in life and joyfully sharing them with those who do not have the basic necessities of life.

Millions of people in the world do not everything they need in terms of adequate food, clothing, shelter, medical care, and employment opportunities. In Paul's time the people living in Jerusalem were starving because of inadequate food supplies. So Paul reminds the Corinthians and us that God has blessed us with all we need and more. Therefore, we should be so filled with gratitude to God that we will share with those in need joyfully and generously.

A man once asked me: "Why doesn't God feed all those millions of hungry people in the world? Why does God let them starve to death?" I responded by saying: "I think God asks us the same question. Why don't we feed all those millions of hungry people in the world? Why do we let them starve to death?" God has already provided us with all we need to feed all the hungry people in the world. We have the food, the technology, and the capacity to feed all the people in the world and educate and empower them to become self-sustaining. We only lack the will and commitment to do so.

So rather than asking why doesn't God or someone else feed them, Paul focuses our attention on the blessings God has already given us. Then, because we are so grateful for the blessings in our lives, we will want to share joyfully and generously with those in need in our world.

Joy Is the Infallible Sign of the Presence of God

A friend once gave me a plaque with this phrase: "Joy is the infallible sign of the presence of God." This phrase has been attributed to the French Priest and Scientist, Father Pierre Teilhard de Chardin.

As a scientist, Teilhard de Chardin spent his life looking for signs of God in the natural world and found them in abundance. When he found such signs of God he was filled with joy and concluded that whenever we experience deep joy it is an infallible sign that we are in the presence of our living God.

Paul also reminds us that joy and generosity are included as fruits of the spirit. In Galatians 5:22-23 Paul writes, "The fruit of the Spirit is love, joy, peace, patience, kindness, generosity, faithfulness, gentleness, and self-control" (NRSV).

One of the ways we can determine if the spirit of God is living in and through us is to ask ourselves:

"Is love the motivating force in my life?"

"Am I characterized as a joy-filled person?"

"Do I live in peace with God and others around me?"

"Am I patient with others?"

"Am I kind?"

"Am I generous with my time, talent, and treasure?"

"Am I faithful to God?"

"Am I gentle with others?"

"Do I have self-control of my ego?"

Paul lists love as the first sign of the presence of God's spirit in us. Jesus said the greatest commandment of all is "to love." Our love is to go in two directions: First to "love the Lord your God with all your heart, with all your being, and with all your mind" and second to "love your neighbor as you love yourself" (Matt 22:37-39).

We love God first and allow God's love to flow in us and through us to all those around us. Then we experience the present of deep joy in our lives, peace in our souls, and our outward actions are characterized by patience, kindness, gentleness, generosity, faithfulness, and control of our ego.

A camp song seeks to unite some of these spiritual qualities with creative images: "I've got peace like a river in my soul. / I've got love like an ocean in my soul. / I've got joy like a fountain in my soul. / I've got hope like a rainbow in my soul."[1] Since our lives are shaped by what we think about and sing about, our intention is that peace, love, joy, and hope will become realities in our lives as we focus on these spiritual gifts.

In John 15, Jesus said, "I have said these things to you so that my joy will be in you and your joy will be complete. This is my commandment: love each other just as I have loved you" (vv. 11-12).

Jesus made it clear that when we love each other completely as he first loved us, we experience the same deep and abiding joy that he experienced. Joy is not a quality we can seek. Joy is the by-product or result of loving others deeply as Christ has loved us.

When we love others deeply and completely, we experience great joy in our hearts and it is out of this joy that we give generously and become "cheerful givers."

Jesus said that he wanted his "joy [to] be in you [so that] your joy will be complete" (John 15:11).

Jesus characterized himself as a joyful person and he wanted his followers to experience the same joy that he experienced. The joy of Jesus comes from his deep, total love for, and trust in, God. His joy was based on what was inside him and not on outward circumstances.

One of my favorite paintings of Jesus is Ralph Kozak's *Jesus Laughing*. It shows Jesus with his head thrown back in laughter. Jesus trusted his life and his future completely into the hands of God and let go of fear, anxiety, and worry. When we trust God completely regardless of our circumstances and "let go and let God," we open ourselves up to the possibility of living joyfully as Jesus did. Jesus said he gave us the commandments to trust God and love God and others so that "my joy will be in you and your joy will be complete."

Norman Cousins was an American political journalist, author, and professor. Late in his life Cousins was diagnosed with a very painful and life-threatening form of arthritis and given little chance of surviving. While he was in a hospital he could only become pain free with high doses of pain medication that virtually knocked him out.

Cousins discovered that when old friends came to see him and they told humorous stories from the past that caused him to laugh, he would be pain free for a few hours. He concluded that laughter was indeed the best medicine. So he checked himself out of a hospital and into a hotel where he developed his own recovery program based on living with a positive attitude, love, faith, hope, and laughter.

Cousins would play old Marx Brothers comedy films and discovered that a few moments of laughter could give him hours of pain-free sleep. In his book *Anatomy of an Illness* he wrote, "I made the joyous discovery that ten minutes of genuine belly laughter had an anesthetic effect and would give me at least two hours of pain-free sleep. When the pain-killing effect of the laughter wore off, we would switch on the motion-picture projector again, and, not infrequently, it would lead to another pain-free sleep interval."[2] Cousins discovered that when he lived with an attitude of gratitude and counted his blessings; expressed his faith, hope, and love; and could laugh at humorous events or old comedy movies, it lifted his spirits and gave him hours of pain-free sleep. Eventually, Cousins became pain free and lived much longer than anyone expected him to live.

Living with the inner attitudes of gratitude, faith, hope, love, and laughter have a positive effect on our bodies, minds, and souls.

Joy is based on what is happening within us. Happiness is based on what happens outside of us. When we are surrounded by pleasant and comfortable conditions and by people we love, we may feel a sense of happiness. But when those conditions change and our loved ones are gone, our happiness also disappears.

Joy is not based on our outward conditions. Joy is an inner state of a trusting and loving relationship with the God who dwells within each of us.

Our outward conditions may be pleasant or difficult but our inner source of joy is constant regardless of what is happening around us.

George Matheson was a nineteenth-century Scottish clergyman. When he was twenty years old he discovered he was going blind and there was nothing the doctors could do about it. He was engaged to be married at the time and when his fiancée found out about his impending blindness, she broke off the engagement because she did not feel she could go through life married to a blind man. Matheson was heartbroken but continued to study for the ministry, was ordained as a pastor, and served parishes for thirty-one years in spite of his blindness.

While he had lost his sight and the love of his life, he knew that the love of God would never leave him, so he wrote the hymn "O Love That Wilt Not Let Me Go":

> O Love that wilt not let me go,
> I rest my weary soul in thee;
> I give thee back the life I owe,
> that in thine ocean depths its flow
> may richer, fuller be.

The third verse of this hymn speaks about a joy that seeks us through pain, and it has made a profound difference in my life:

> O Joy that seekest me through pain,
> I cannot close my heart to thee;
> I trace the rainbow thru the rain,
> and feel the promise is not vain,
> that morn shall tearless be.[3]

I am amazed that a man who lost the love of his life and his eyesight could affirm that God's joy was still seeking him through the pain and he could still "trace the rainbow through the rain."

I once came across this verse when I was going through a painful time in my life. I was the lead pastor on a church staff where there was conflict among staff members. The harder I tried to manage the conflict the worse it became. It was a painful and difficult time for me.

I wanted to avoid this pain. However, in George Matheson's hymn I sang: "O Joy that seekest me through pain." It had never occurred to me that joy could be seeking me through my pain. I saw my pain in a different light when I thought that God's joy was on the other side of my pain.

When I faced the darkness of pain directly, accepted it, and walked through it with God, I discovered a new depth of joy in my life. Joy was seeking me through pain.

Joy often seeks us through pain. A mother goes through the painful experience of childbirth and afterwards is filled with joy over the birth of a new baby. A person may go through the painful experience of major surgery and afterwards experience joy through improved physical capacities. Joy often seeks us through pain.

When we are in a painful situation, we try to close our hearts to pain, to ignore it and hope that it will go away. Matheson reminds us that when we open our hearts to the painful experiences in life, accept them, and walk through them, we will come into the light and joy of God on the other side.

Even in the midst of the painful times Matheson wrote, "I trace the rainbow thru the rain, and feel the promise is not vain, that morn shall tearless be."

In the midst of the rains of pain that come into our lives, we are challenged to look for the rainbow of joy on the other side of the rain and know that the sun will come up again tomorrow and "morn shall tearless be."

Psalm 23 also reminds us that when we "walk through the darkest valley," we can "fear no danger because you are with [us]" (v. 4).

When we walk through the dark valleys of life, there is nothing to fear because God walks with us and will lead us through the valley of the shadow of death into the meadow of light and joy. A friend reminded me that God leads us through the darkest valleys of life; we are not to pitch our tent and camp out in the dark valleys but to walk with God through them.

The faithful followers of Jesus live with a deep and abiding joy regardless of the circumstances around us because we know we don't walk alone and we know that even in the painful parts of life God walks with us and leads us to deeper experiences of joy.

Unfortunately, the followers of Jesus are not always characterized by the presence of love and joy in their lives.

Recently a survey of unchurched people revealed that most people who do not have any religious affiliation do not feel that Christians are characterized by love and joy.

People without any religious affiliation were asked to describe what they felt Christians are like. They described Christians as people who seemed angry, judgmental, and self-righteous. When asked how they formed this opinion about Christians, they often referred to the preachers they have seen on television who are frequently judgmental toward people who do not believe as they do and are generally angry in the attitude they project.

Unfortunately, when a new person enters a local congregation for the first time, they often report there is a somber, depressing mood rather than an attitude of joy, expectation, hope, love, and gratitude.

However, this is not the attitude of the Christ we follow. Jesus wanted his joy to live in and through us to bring joy and love to all those around us. It is true that joy is an infallible sign of the presence of God and if we do not allow Christ's joy and love to live in us then it is obvious that God is not present in our lives.

Joy is the infallible sign of the presence of God, and people who are filled with the presence of God give cheerfully and joyfully to God.

Joy to the World

During the Christmas season, we sing "Joy to the World" because we believe God sent Jesus to bring joy into the world. When we experience the joy of Jesus in our lives, we give ourselves cheerfully and joyfully to God.

Isaac Watts based his hymn "Joy to the World" on Psalm 98:4-9:

> Shout triumphantly to the LORD, all the earth!
>> Be happy!
>> Rejoice out loud!
>> Sing your praises!
> Sing your praises to the LORD with the lyre—
>> with the lyre and the sound of music.
> With trumpets and a horn blast,
>> shout triumphantly before the LORD, the king!
> . . . .
> Let all the rivers clap their hands;
>> let the mountains rejoice out loud altogether before the LORD
>> because he is coming to establish justice on the earth.

The psalmist invites the followers of God to "shout triumphantly" and "rejoice out loud" to thank God for the living presence of God in our world.

Isaac Watts affirms that because God sent Jesus into the world we sing joyously:

> Joy to the World, the Lord is come!
> Let earth receive her King;

Let every heart prepare him room,
And heaven and nature sing.[4]

When we open up and receive God's unconditional love that comes to us in Jesus Christ, our hearts are filled full to overflowing with love and joy. And we give back to God out of the overflow.

Sometimes we feel that if we give generously to God, then we will have less for ourselves. If we give God some of our time, talent, and treasure, we will have less time, talent, and treasure to use as we choose.

But the truth is that when we open up and receive God's abundant love into our lives, we are overfilled with love, joy, and blessings. So we give to God joyfully and cheerfully out of the overflow of the blessings in our lives. We don't have less; we have more because we can't outgive God. God always gives far more to us than we give back to God.

I once led a funeral for an eighty-eight-year-old therapist who lived her life fully and joyfully. She was so filled with life and love that clients continued to seek her out for counseling when she was eighty-five years old. During her memorial service, former clients, colleagues, and students shared how much they felt her love and joy for them and for life. They told stories about how she had listened so carefully and loved so deeply that they were transformed by her loving and joyful spirit.

She wanted her memorial service to be a celebration of her life and a joyful experience for everyone. So she requested that a friend of hers who was a professional dancer dance in the aisles at her service while a jazz band played "In the Mood." When the dancer started dancing, people started clapping and laughing and eventually some got up and danced as well. Her request was fulfilled and the service was an experience of celebrating her loving and joyful life.

She poured herself out in loving service to God and to others, and in return she was filled full to overflowing with love, joy, and enthusiasm for life and eternal life. She gave herself totally to loving and caring for others and wanted her memorial service to be an occasion for joy and celebration of the life she had been privileged to live.

When we open our lives up to God, God fills all of us full to overflowing with enthusiasm, passion for life, love, and joy so we want to give time, talent, and treasure back to God with a cheerful and joyful heart.

When we walk the Gratitude Path in life, there is a smile on our face because we are filled full to overflowing with joy in our hearts. We become the cheerful givers whom God loves. As Paul says: "God loves a cheerful giver" (2 Cor 9:7).

Questions for Discussion

1. Do I give to God out of obligation, guilt, or a need to meet the church budget, or do I give to God cheerfully out of a grateful heart?

2. Is my life characterized by joy and generosity?

3. When I am going through a painful time, can I see the joy beyond the pain, trace the rainbow through the rain?

4. Do I demonstrate the fruits of the spirit: love, joy, peace, patience, kindness, generosity, faithfulness, gentleness, and self-control?

EXPECT A MIRACLE

Jesus was unable to do many miracles there because of their disbelief.

—Matthew 13:58

Nothing is impossible for God.

—Luke 1:37

Either everything is a miracle or nothing is.

—Albert Einstein

When we walk the Gratitude Path of counting our many blessings from God, we discover that God is alive and still works miracles in our world.

The Oxford Dictionary defines a miracle as "a surprising and welcome event that is not explicable by natural or scientific laws and is therefore considered to be the work of a divine agency."[1]

As followers of Jesus we believe that he performed many miracles or "surprising and welcome" events during his ministry here on earth. The Gospels are full of stories about Jesus healing persons who were paralyzed, blind or deaf, mentally ill, or afflicted with leprosy. We also believe that God performed the greatest miracle of all in raising Jesus from death to life.

However, we often have a hard time believing that God continues to perform surprising and welcome events that cannot be explained by natural or scientific laws today. We have a hard time believing that God still performs miracles. We have become so logical and rational that if someone claims to have experienced a miracle we often doubt it and think there must be some other rational explanation.

In Matthew 13 we are told that Jesus went to his hometown of Nazareth and taught in their synagogue on the Sabbath. The people who had known Jesus from the time he was a little boy were astonished by his wisdom and his miracles and said, "'Where did he get this wisdom? Where did he get the power to work miracles? Isn't he the carpenter's son? Isn't his mother named Mary? Aren't James, Joseph, Simon, and Judas his brothers? And his sisters, aren't they here with us? Where did this man get all this?' They were repulsed by him and fell into sin" (vv. 54-57).

Luke's Gospel adds that the people of Nazareth were so offended at Jesus that they "ran him out of town. They led him to the crest of the hill on which their town had been built so that they could throw him off the cliff. But he passed through the crowd and went on his way" (Luke 4:29-30).

Matthew concludes this story of Jesus's rejection at Nazareth with the words: "He was unable to do many miracles there because of their disbelief" (Matt 13:58).

Jesus did not perform many miracles in his own hometown "because of their disbelief." People did not believe in God's ability to work miracles through Jesus and he did few miracles there. When people did not believe in his ability to perform miracles, fewer miracles were performed. Jesus performed many healing miracles in nearby Cana of Galilee; in Capernaum, Jericho, and Jerusalem; and around the sea of Galilee, but he did few miracles in Nazareth "because of their disbelief."

Undoubtedly, there were more people who were sick, paralyzed, blind, and deaf in Nazareth as well, but Jesus did few miracles in his hometown of Nazareth "because of their disbelief."

I wonder how many miracles are not performed in our cities and towns "because of [our] disbelief." Like the people of Nazareth, many church leaders don't believe in God's power to perform miracles so we don't experience the surprising and welcome miracles that God would like to give us.

In our secular world people often say that they won't believe it until they see it. They have to see it to believe it. However, the truth is that we have to believe in miracles before we will see them happen. Belief comes first.

"[Jesus] was unable to do many miracles there because of their disbelief." Presumably, if the people of Nazareth had believed in Christ's power to perform miracles, more miracles of healing would have occurred in Nazareth just as they occurred in all the other towns Jesus visited.

A miracle is simply another blessing from God for which we give God thanks and praise.

Many years ago, Lyle Schaller developed a fund-raising plan called "Miracle Sunday."[2] Schaller described a Miracle Sunday as an opportunity for people to experience the miracle of generosity by giving on one Sunday what they might give in a two- or three-year capital campaign. When Schaller first announced this plan, many people thought the idea of raising such a large amount of money on one Sunday was utterly impossible.

However, congregational leaders who believed "with God all things are possible" discovered they could enroll their people in the vision of Miracle Sunday and trust God to work the miracle of generosity in ways they never could have imagined.

Over the past thirty years, dozens of congregations have raised an amount of money equal to one-third to three times the size of the church's annual operating budget through the Miracle Sunday program.

I have participated in Miracle Sunday campaigns in four different congregations of vastly different sizes and always with amazing results.

When I was appointed to serve First United Methodist Church in Sioux Falls, South Dakota, the church had just completed a building campaign to build a new education wing and install a new pipe organ. The expenses for the new building and organ exceeded the amount pledged by two hundred thousand dollars.

Our finance committee was reluctant to conduct another three-year pledge drive, so they asked me if I had any suggestions. I had read about the Miracle Sunday campaign, so I suggested that we receive a special offering on one Sunday to receive two hundred thousand dollars and pay off the debt.

The finance chairperson looked at me as if he thought I had lost my mind! He explained that he knew well the giving patterns of our congregation and he was positive that there was no way we could raise two hundred thousand dollars on one Sunday.

I said to our finance chairperson: "Would it be a miracle if we did raise two hundred thousand dollars on one Sunday?" He replied, "It would take a miracle from God for such a thing to happen in our congregation." I reminded him that we are people of faith who believe in miracles and that with God all things are possible.

The finance committee decided to give Miracle Sunday a try even though most of them did not believe it would happen but whatever we raised would help pay down the debt on our facilities.

We decided to do the campaign during Lent of that year and receive the Miracle Sunday offering on Palm Sunday. Each Sunday in Lent I preached about miracles and how God still works miracles in our world today.

One Sunday morning a young couple shared their story with the congregation. They had been married for ten years and had been told by many fertility specialists that they would never be able to conceive and bear a child. As they told their story they were holding their three-month-old daughter in their arms and crying. Their doctor told them this was a "miracle baby" because he had been convinced that they would never be able to conceive and bear a child.

Another Sunday morning an older man shared with the congregation that he had been told he had incurable cancer and had about a year to live. The man smiled broadly and said, "That was ten years ago." He explained that every time he visited his doctor for a checkup, his doctor would shake his head and simply say, "It must be a miracle."

This does not mean that every infertile couple will conceive and bear a child or that every cancer patient will outlive their diagnosis, but it does mean that we always have to be open to the possibility that God is still working miracles in the world.

I asked our congregation just to believe that God could work the miracle of generosity among us, to pray for a miracle, to give whatever they felt God called them to give, and then to accept whatever miracle God wanted to give.

Our chief unbeliever was the chair of our finance committee. When people would ask him if he thought we could raise two hundred thousand dollars on one Sunday, He would say, "No, but whatever we raise will help." I asked him if he just wouldn't say "no." I asked him to say "maybe" or "possibly." I just wanted him to have a mustard-seed size faith and leave open the door that God could work a miracle among us. We had no guarantee that it would happen, but we just had to believe that it was possible because "with God all things are possible."

About a week before Miracle Sunday, the finance chairperson called me to tell me that something was happening to him. He was starting to believe that it might be possible for us to reach this goal. His rational mind told him it was impossible but his heart told him it just might happen. I felt the miracle had already happened because our finance chair believed it was possible!

A Lutheran woman in our community heard about our Miracle Sunday project and sent a very generous check to the church with a note saying: "I have always wanted to be a part of a miracle." The Baptist pastor called and told me that he and his congregation would be praying for the miracle of generosity on our Miracle Sunday because "the world needs more miracles." When Miracle Sunday arrived, I told our congregation that a

Lutheran woman had sent a generous check and a Baptist congregation was praying for us. When we receive Lutheran gifts and Baptist prayers to help a Methodist church pay off its debt, a miracle has already happened!

The Miracle Sunday offering was received early in each service and sent to the office to be counted. At the end of the third service, our lay leader glided down the center aisle with a smile on her face and a slip of paper in her hand. I announced the results to the congregation: "Today our Miracle Sunday offering is $210,000!" God has given us a miracle. Thanks be to God." We sang "To God Be the Glory," and people had tears in their eyes.

Our hearts were filled full to overflowing with thanksgiving and gratitude to God because it was clear to all of us that God had been at work among us to engender this kind of generosity on one Sunday.

I will have to confess that I was totally overwhelmed. I believed that with God all things are possible but I was overjoyed at the surprising and welcome event (a miracle) that had happened before our very eyes.

One of the most significant results of Miracle Sunday was the growth in the faith of the people in the congregation. Not only were funds raised, but faith was raised as well. Worship attendance increased significantly. People wanted to come to the place where God had performed a miracle. Bible study attendance increased as people wanted to know more about this God who still works miracles today. New Prayer groups formed to teach people how to pray to God, trust in God, and accept whatever gifts God wants to give us.

This experience deepened my own faith in God. I became more consistently faithful in my own prayer time. I took my prayers for others more seriously and trusted God to work miracles in God's own time and way.

I also realized that the hardest part of Miracle Sunday was getting people to believe in the possibility of miracles. We live in such a cynical, negative, and angry atmosphere that it is hard to convince even the followers of Jesus to trust in God completely and that God can still transform our world into a compassionate, inclusive, just, and Christlike community.

Lyle Schaller suggests two factors are critical to Miracle Sunday success: (1) Establish one, two, or three causes or needs that almost everyone in the congregation will support enthusiastically. (2) Set a goal for Miracle Sunday that is more than one-third of the church's annual budget.[3] A smaller goal does not stimulate the imagination of the people and make us realize that we will need to depend on God for success. Additional guidelines for Miracle Sunday can be found in Wayne C. Barrett's *The Church Finance Idea Book*.[4]

When we walk the Gratitude Path, we discover that God still works miracles in our world and gives us even more reasons to give thanks to God and sing God's praises.

I wonder if the author of Psalm 100 had experienced some surprising and welcome event in his life that caused him to write:

> Shout triumphantly to the LORD, all the earth!
> Serve the LORD with celebration!
> Come before him with shouts of joy!
> . . . .
> Enter his gates with thanks;
>   enter his courtyards with praise!
> Thank him! Bless his name!
> Because the LORD is good,
>   his loyal love lasts forever;
>   his faithfulness lasts generation after generation. (vv. 1-2, 4-5)

Whenever we experience the surprising and welcome events in our lives that we call miracles, we too want to make a joyful noise to the Lord and give thanks to God and bless God's name.

Praying for Healing Miracles

Congregations where people give joyfully and generously to support God's work are also congregations that provide a high level of loving pastoral care to the people in the congregation and community. Some stewardship leaders maintain that the best stewardship program is an active and effective pastoral and congregational care program for parishioners in the congregation. When people in a congregation experience the love of God in their lives in a personal way through good pastoral care, they want to give generously to support God's work out of gratitude for the loving care they have received.

One of the ways pastors and congregational leaders can provide good pastoral care is through praying for people in their times of need.

The Gospel of Matthew summarizes the ministry of Jesus with these words: "Jesus traveled throughout Galilee, teaching in their synagogues. He announced the good news of the kingdom and healed every disease and sickness among the people....People brought to him all those who had various kinds of diseases, those in pain, those possessed by demons, those with epilepsy, and those who were paralyzed, and he healed them" (Matt 4:23-24).

Matthew tells us that Jesus went about Galilee doing three things: teaching, preaching, and healing. Faithful congregations today continue to follow Jesus by teaching through our educational ministries; preaching in our worship services; and praying for healing in body, mind, and soul.

However, followers of Jesus are often more comfortable teaching about God and preaching the good news than they are about praying for the healing of the sick. So many people who have prayed that God would heal someone who ended up dying feel that their prayer was not answered in the way they wanted it to be answered. So they may be reluctant to pray for God to heal someone. Furthermore, people are often distrustful of television preachers who claim to be faith healers, so they are reluctant to actively pray for God's healing power when someone is sick.

The followers of Jesus recognize that Jesus touched or spoke to sick people and they were healed, but frequently that is not our experience today. So how are we to pray to God for the miracle of healing in our lives or the lives of those we love?

We need to recognize that prayer is basically making a request of God. When we make a request of God, we can't determine how it will be answered; God will decide that. God may respond to our prayer requests by saying yes, or no, or maybe, or later. We can't determine God's response; we simply make our heartfelt requests to our compassionate and loving God.

I have discovered that God often responds to our prayers for healing requests in one of four different ways.

First, sometimes when we pray for someone God may provide immediate improvement or complete healing. In my experience, immediate healings are very rare but they sometimes occur.

Rev. John Blacker was an Australian pastor who once came to preach at a weeklong series of services in a church I served. Rev. Blacker believed strongly in the power of God to heal through prayer and took seriously Christ's command to "heal the sick."

A woman in our congregation called the church and asked if Rev. Blacker would come to her home and pray for her husband. She explained that he had terrible back problems and had been to see many different medical doctors but could get no relief from his pain. The woman explained that her husband was not a man of faith and never came to worship with her.

I explained the situation to Rev. Blacker and he said, "Let's go pray for God to heal him."

When we arrived at her home, her husband was sitting in a recliner in obvious pain. I introduced Rev. Blacker to him and told him we came to pray for his healing. The husband replied: "I'd do anything to get some relief from this pain."

Rev. Blacker went around behind him, laid his hands on his shoulders, and simply prayed, "God, thank you for this healing." Then he stood there with his hands on the man's shoulders praying silently for about ten minutes.

I saw tears running down the man's cheeks. After a while Rev. Blacker prayed again, "God, thank you for this healing."

We sat in silence for a few moments and then the man opened his eyes, got up out of his chair, walked around the room, and simply said, "It's gone. The pain is gone." We joined hands together and offered a prayer of thanksgiving to God. Then Rev. Blacker and I rushed back to the church for the evening service.

I was astounded. I had never witnessed someone being healed from serious pain immediately through prayer. Rev. Blacker explained that it is rare but since it sometimes happens it makes us take prayer much more seriously when we realize that God could use us as a channel of God's healing power and give people immediate relief.

I will have to confess that I wondered if this healing would last or if his pain might return again soon. About a week after his healing, the man stopped by the church office to thank me for bringing Rev. Blacker to his house and to thank God for his healing. He told me he was on his way to help his son reroof his house. I said, "Then you are still pain free?" He looked at me and said, "Kent, I am completely healed, O ye of little faith!"

This healing experience completely changed his life. He became a faithful follower of Jesus and a generous supporter of God's ministry through the church. While it is rare, sometimes God may heal a person quickly and completely through prayers for healing and it can transform their lives.

This experience had a profound effect on me and my ministry. After this experience, whenever someone asked me to pray for them or for someone they loved, I would stop whatever I was doing, take their hand in mine, and offer a brief prayer requesting God's healing for them or their loved one. I have prayed for people in the narthex of the church, at a grocery store or post office, or even at a basketball game. If God can use our prayers to bring relief to suffering people, I want to be available to request God's healing power any time or any place prayer is requested.

The second way God often responds to prayers for healing is that the healing may come gradually over time. God heals gradually through the love and prayers of people and through the competent and compassionate care of medical doctors, nurses, treatments, and medications.

Dr. Larry Dossey, in his book *Healing Words: The Power of Prayer and the Practice of Medicine*, maintains that good medical care combined with the loving prayer of family, friends, and even strangers is more effective in bringing about healing than simply good medical care alone. Dr. Larry Dossey is former Chief of Staff of Medical City Dallas Hospital in Texas. Dr. Dossey did not believe in the power of prayer to assist healing until he started to notice that his patients who had people praying for them seemed to heal faster than those who did not have people praying for them. He also discovered that there have been over fifty scientific experiments that showed that prayer brings about significant changes in the healing process.[5]

Dr. Dossey reported on a study done by Dr. Randolph Byrd, a cardiologist at San Francisco General Hospital, on patients admitted to the coronary care unit of the hospital where he practiced. A computer assigned 393 cardiac patients randomly to either a group that was prayed for by home prayer groups or to a group that was not intentionally remembered in prayer. Prayer groups were just given the first name and a brief description of their condition for the patients they were to pray for each day.

At the end of ten months, the results of this study were tabulated and the positive effect of prayer was documented. The prayed-for group was five times less likely to require antibiotics and three times less likely to develop pulmonary edema than the nonprayed-for group. None of the prayed-for group required endotracheal intubation (being put on a ventilator) while twelve of the unremembered group required ventilator support.[6]

After the results of this study were reported, Dr. William Nolan, who had written a book debunking faith healing wrote: "It sounds like this study will stand up to scrutiny....maybe we doctors ought to be writing on our order sheets, 'Pray three times a day.' If it works, it works."[7]

As a result of studying scientific experiments that revealed the positive effect of prayer and good medical treatment Dr. Dossey decided that he would pray for his patients daily. "I would go to my office earlier than usual each morning, ceremoniously light incense, and enter a prayerful, meditative frame of mind. As the incense filed the room, I would invoke the Absolute, asking only that 'thy will be done' in the lives of the patients I was about to see that day...Was I a better doctor as a result of it? I do not know. I believe the answer is yes, if for no other reason than that I felt more connected with those I served."[8]

When we pray for healing for someone, sometimes God answers through the combination of good medical treatment and loving prayers for healing.

In the Gospels sometimes healings also take place gradually. Luke tells a story about a man who has been beaten almost to death by robbers and left beside the road between Jerusalem and Jericho to die (Luke 10:29-37). A compassionate Samaritan came along and poured oil and wine on the man's wounds, which was the best medical treatment known at that time. The Samaritan then took the injured man to an inn, paid for his room and board, and asked the innkeeper to look after him while he was gone.

The assumption is that the man was not healed immediately but was healed gradually over time. When we offer good pastoral care and prayers for people today, their healing also may come gradually over time.

A woman in our congregation had diabetes that had caused her to lose sight in one eye. A medical doctor who was an eye specialist explained to her that her diabetes caused "floaters" or weakened veins in her eyes. One of those floaters had burst, which caused her to go blind in one eye. The doctor could see other floaters in her good eye and would treat them so they wouldn't burst and cause blindness in her good eye. However, he said her condition was getting worse and eventually one of those floaters would burst and she would be completely blind.

At one of our prayers for healing services, she asked the group to pray for her healing so that she did not go blind. We all laid hands on her and each offered a prayer requesting God's healing for her eye. Jan felt nothing immediately and said she could still see floaters in her good eye.

However, the next time she went to see her doctor, he noticed that there were fewer floaters in her eye than the visit before. A month later, there were even fewer floaters and eventually there were no floaters in her eye at all. The doctor said he had never seen a case where this condition reversed itself. She explained that people in her congregation had been praying for her healing, but the doctor remained mystified over this scientifically unexplained healing

This woman was extremely grateful for these prayers of healing that allowed her to continue to see. She lives with a deep feeling of gratitude to God and those who prayed for her and is a faithful and generous supporter of God's work through her congregation.

The third way God responds to our prayers for healing is that God does not give physical healing at all but provides the grace to live victoriously in the midst of the illness.

St. Paul had what he called a "thorn in [his] body," (2 Cor 12:7) which was some chronic medical condition that caused him pain all his life. Paul said he prayed three times for God to heal him of his physical affliction but he was not physically healed.

Rather, God told Paul, "My grace is enough for you, because power is made perfect in weakness" (v. 9).

Paul was not healed of his physical affliction but he was given the grace to live victoriously with his illness. Even though Paul carried this illness all his life, God gave him the grace to live with it and used him to start and support Christian churches all over the Mediterranean and to write half of the New Testament.

Sometimes when we pray for someone's healing, they are not healed physically but are given the grace to live victoriously in spite of their illness.

I once knew a woman who lived with painful arthritis for most of her life. She came to our healing prayer group where we laid hands on her and prayed for her physical healing. Afterward, she was ecstatic. She walked around praising God and thanking everyone in the prayer group.

I asked her if her arthritis was better. She said, "No, it still hurts like always, but isn't God wonderful?"

She was not healed physically from her pain but, like Paul, she was filled with the love and grace of God so she could live victoriously in spite of her painful condition. Sometimes when we pray for someone's healing, they may not be healed at all but are given the grace to live victoriously with the illness.

Finally, the fourth way God may respond to our prayers for healing is to give us the ultimate healing, the union of our spirits with the spirit of God. The truth is that even if we are healed physically of some disease today, eventually our physical bodies will wear out and die and then we will be reunited with the God who created us in the first place.

Everyone Jesus healed in the Gospels, died eventually. All physical healing is penultimate. The ultimate healing of our lives comes when we let go of these physical bodies and are reunited with our loving creator, God.

My dad died of cancer. One day I sat beside his bed in an intensive care unit of a hospital. Suddenly, he opened his eyes, looked at me, and said, "I just saw my dad." I replied, "Your dad died thirty years ago." He said, "I just saw him!" "Where?" I asked. He said, "Over in that bright light" and motioned to the corner of the hospital room where he could see a bright light that I could not see.

Dad laid his head back on the pillow and said, "I can see myself going to join him. But I am not going for two days." He glowed as he said this as if he was looking into the light of eternity.

That was on a Wednesday at noon. Two days later on Friday he entered that eternal light.

Looking back on it we realized why he waited. My older sister, was on a trip to Europe. I called her and told her that Dad was not doing well and she needed to return home. She arrived on Friday. She came into his room; they hugged, kissed, and cried; and I offered a prayer. Within five minutes after I prayed that prayer, Dad entered that eternal light.

This experience of my dad's death was confirmation for me that what Jesus said is true: "My Father's house has room to spare....When I go to prepare a place for you, I will return and take you with me so that what I am you will be too" (John 14:2-3).

When we pray for people in need, God may respond with immediate healing, gradual healing, the grace to live victoriously with the illness, or the ultimate healing of life, which is union with God. Good pastoral care is praying for people and surrendering people into the loving hands of God regardless of how God may respond.

I have discovered that pastors and congregations that provide good, loving, prayerful pastoral care to their members, have fewer financial concerns than those congregations where people do not experience God's love and compassion through the pastors or congregational leaders.

To put it another way, no stewardship plan or program will be effective, if the people of a congregation do not experience God's love and care through the love and care of the pastor and leaders of the congregation.

When we provide loving pastoral care in a congregation, people will thank God for God's living presence in their lives and walk the Gratitude Path that leads to the garden of generosity.

Discussion Questions

1. Have you or someone you know ever experienced a surprising and welcome event called a miracle?

2. Do you believe God still performs miracles in our world?

3. Have you ever experienced loving care from the pastor or people in your congregation during a time of need?

4. Do you help provide loving care to people in need in your congregation?

CHAPTER SIX

LEADING A GRATITUDE CAMPAIGN

We want you to excel also in this generous undertaking.
—2 Corinthians 8:7 NRSV

They gave what they could afford and even more than they could afford, and they did it voluntarily. . . . They even exceeded our expectations, because they gave themselves to the Lord first.
—2 Corinthians 8:3, 5

In Paul's second letter to the Christians in Corinth, Paul encourages the Corinthians to give generously to support the Christians in Jerusalem who were facing a severe famine. Paul told the Corinthians that the Christians in Macedonia had already responded to his appeal and had given generously and even beyond their means to care for others in need.

Paul wanted the followers of Jesus in Corinth to "excel also in this generous undertaking" (2 Cor 8:7 NRSV).

My hope and prayer is that your congregation will also excel in generating generosity for God's work through practicing the principles of a Gratitude Campaign or a Miracle Sunday capital campaign.

I have conducted Gratitude Campaigns in about two dozen congregations of all sizes throughout the Midwest. My experience has been that when pastors and congregations follow these principles they experience joy in giving and an increase in the number of people who made commitments and in the total income pledged to support God's work in their congregation.

One congregation reported to me that this Gratitude Campaign had generated about a third more in commitments and a third more in total income to support God's work through their congregation for the next year. But more than that, they discovered that people who had never made a commitment to the church before made commitments because the focus was on counting their blessings and not on talking about the needs of the church.

I have also led several Miracle Sunday capital campaigns in local congregations, which led to unexpected generosity for local church capital needs. One small-town congregation surprised themselves in generating over $50,000 of giving on the Sunday before Christmas to repair their pipe organ that had become no longer usable. That congregation, which did not have a history of generous giving, grew in faith and commitment when they realized that God had worked the miracle of generosity in their midst. See chapter 5 for more details about a Miracle Sunday capital campaign.

The Gratitude Campaign process is based on the Christian belief that God has been exceedingly generous to all of us and we are deeply grateful for all these blessings. It is out of gratitude for all God has done for us that we joyfully give our time, talent, and treasure to God as an expression of our gratitude to God.

The Gratitude Campaign

Here is a step-by-step outline of principles for conducting a Gratitude Campaign in your congregation.

1. Share the Gratitude Path free brochure with your local church finance committee, administrative council, or governing board. Explain the theology of a Gratitude Campaign as encouraging people to count all the blessings they have received from God and to give time, talent, and treasure to God out of gratitude for all God has first done for them. A Gratitude Campaign focuses on God and our gratitude for all God has done for us and does not focus on the needs of a local congregation. Therefore, we give to support God's work through the church out of our personal gratitude not out of obligation, guilt, or the need to meet the church budget. Invite the leaders of your congregation to adopt this model for developing an attitude of gratitude in your congregation and for your local church stewardship campaign.

2. Invite the pastor and other adult Sunday school teachers to lead a five-week study of the book *The Gratitude Path: Leading Your Church to Generosity* at any time during the year or during the five weeks before you celebrate Gratitude Sunday in your congregation. Chapters 1–4 of *The Gratitude Path* provide a biblical foundation and practical illustrations for a local church annual stewardship campaign based on our gratitude to God. Chapter 5 provides information and guidance for leading a Miracle Sunday short-term capital campaign to generate immediate gifts for a widely recognized capital need in a local congregation.

3. Schedule a date for Gratitude Sunday.

   Many congregations schedule the Sunday before Thanksgiving for Gratitude Sunday. The Thanksgiving season is a time when people in the United States already focus their attention on giving thanks to God for all their blessings in life. Furthermore, more people frequently attend worship services on the Sunday before Thanksgiving so more people are likely to be in worship to participate in the Gratitude Campaign. However, each congregation should schedule Gratitude Sunday on a date that best fits their local church schedule.

   Congregations have used a variety of theme statements for their Gratitude Campaigns. Some have called it the "Count Your Many Blessings Campaign" or the "Give Thanks with a Grateful Heart Campaign" or "Giving with an Attitude of Gratitude" or "Now Thank We All Our God" or "Praise God from Whom All Blessings Flow" or simply "The Gratitude Path Campaign" or "The Gratitude Campaign." Choose a theme that communicates your gratitude to God for all the blessings in your life.

4. Plan a complementary catered Gratitude Brunch on Gratitude Sunday.

   The purpose of providing a complementary Gratitude Brunch is to give the congregational leaders an opportunity to thank the members of the church for their generosity in supporting God's work through their congregation. In congregations with multiple worship services the brunch can be available all Sunday morning. In congregations with one worship service, the brunch can be available following the worship service. It should not be a potluck brunch because that would require families to prepare and bring food rather than focusing on thanking the congregation for their commitment of time, talent, and treasure to God. The finance committee should pay for the brunch or lunch as their way of thanking the congregation for their support for God's work.

For three or four weeks prior to Gratitude Sunday the congregation should be encouraged to make reservations for the Gratitude Brunch by filling out reservation cards in the bulletin and in church mailings. The goal is to enroll as many people as possible in attending the Gratitude Sunday worship service and brunch.

5. The pastor of the church should preach on God's generosity to us and our gratitude to God for three or four weeks prior to Gratitude Sunday. The hymns for worship should be hymns of gratitude for God's blessings in our lives.

Here are some suggested sermon texts:

A. Luke 17:15-17. This is the story of the ten lepers who were healed but only one returned to give thanks to God for healing. Jesus asked, "Weren't ten men cleansed? Where are the other nine?" Often we are like the other nine; we receive blessings from God but take them for granted and fail to return to say thanks.

B. Luke 6:38. Jesus told his followers, "Give, and it will be given to you. A good portion—packed down, firmly shaken, and overflowing—will fall into your lap." The truth is that God has already put a good measure of blessings in our laps. When we give some of our abundance back to God, we discover that we are blessed again because we can't outgive God.

C. 2 Corinthians 9:7. Paul tells us that we should not give out of obligation or guilt (not reluctantly or under compulsion) for God loves a cheerful giver. The way to give cheerfully is to rejoice in all the blessings God has given us and delight in giving some of our resources back to God out of a deep feeling of gratitude.

D. 2 Corinthians 9:11. Paul reminds us that we have been made rich in every way so that we can be generous in every way. Most people don't think they are rich, but if we have a home to live in, hot running water, an income, a car to drive, food to eat, and access to health care, we are richer than 80 percent of the rest of the people in our world. We are blessed to be a blessing to others.

E. Malachi 3:10. The prophet Malachi reminds us to bring the full tithe to God and "see whether I do not open all the windows of the heavens for you and empty out a blessing until there is enough." Many people count all their charitable giving to God's causes in the world as part of their tithe, but each person should follow their own conscience on tithing.

F. Luke 12:15. Jesus warns us to be on guard against all kinds of greed since our life is not measured in the abundance of our possessions. Generosity is the antidote to the sickness of greed since a person can't be generous and greedy simultaneously.

G. 1 Timothy 6:17-19. Paul tells the rich "to do good, to be rich in the good things they do, to be generous, and to share with others...that way they can take hold of what is truly life." Are we rich in things or rich in doing good works?

H. Luke 21:1-2. Jesus contrasts the gifts of the rich who put large gifts into the temple treasury with the gift of a poor widow who puts in two small copper coins. Her gift is honored because she gave sacrificially.

See the introduction for additional texts for preaching for the Gratitude Campaign.

Here are some hymns that would be appropriate for the worship services leading up to and including Gratitude Sunday:

A. "Count Your Many Blessings"

B. "Now Thank We All Our God"

C. "For the Beauty of the Earth"

D. "Give Thanks with a Grateful Heart"

E. "Many and Great"

F. "Praise God, from Whom All Blessings Flow"

G. "Thank You, Lord"

H. "All Creatures of Our God and King"

I. "Bless Thou the Gifts"

J. "Take My Life, and Let It Be Consecrated"

K. "Lord, Whose Love Through Humble Service"

L. "Sing Praise to God Who Reigns Above"

M. "Guide Me, O Thou Great Jehovah"

N. "O God, Our Help in Ages Past"

6. Invite lay speakers to speak in worship or show videos of congregation members expressing their gratitude to God.

   In one congregation a woman spoke about how her forty-five-year-old husband had a massive heart attack a year earlier and was not expected to live. She thanked the congregation for their healing prayers and she thanked God for her husband's healing. Then with tears in her eyes she pointed to her husband sitting in the congregation and said, "I thank God for you." She said she was so filled with gratitude to God that she was eager to give back to God just to say thank you.

   Some congregations have videotaped children, youth, or adults expressing their gratitude to God and shown several brief stories in their worship services. When laypeople see and hear other laypeople expressing their gratitude to God, it encourages them to think about their own blessings and feelings of gratitude toward God.

7. Invite members of the congregation to keep a Gratitude Journal during the weeks leading up to Gratitude Sunday.

   One congregation gave out small journals to everyone in the congregation as a way to encourage them to write down five things they were thankful for each day during the four weeks prior to Gratitude Sunday. Children were given specially made journals to write down the things for which they were thankful. People were encouraged to share with the pastor what this experience was like for them and she shared some of their reflections in the sermons during the Gratitude Campaign. When we actually write down our many blessings from God, it has a positive effect on our daily lives and attitudes.

8. Send out three letters to the congregation before Gratitude Sunday.

Each letter should announce the date for Gratitude Sunday and Brunch and include a reservation card to be returned if the person or family will be present for the Gratitude Brunch.

The first letter should be written by the pastor and include a scriptural quotation about giving and the pastor's own personal feelings of gratitude to God for the blessings in his or her life. The letter should encourage everyone to count their many blessings from God and keep a Gratitude Journal during the Gratitude month.

The second letter should be written by a highly respected layperson and contain their expressions of gratitude to God for the blessings in their lives. It should also encourage everyone to be present in worship for Gratitude Sunday and for the brunch afterward.

The third letter might be written by a young person or someone who has had an experience of God on a work project or church camp. It would be an opportunity for them to thank God for this life-changing experience. This letter should also include a Gratitude Card and let people know that they should bring it to worship on Gratitude Sunday and fill it out after the message, and then they will come forward and lay it on the altar or Communion table as a personal expression of their gratitude to God.

9. Some congregations have had a donor appreciation reception a week or two before Gratitude Sunday to thank everyone who has given to support God's work through the congregation during the past year. At the reception, the pastor or a lay leader can share some of the ministries of the church that have transformed lives because of the generosity of these donors.

   The donor reception is also a good time to explain that the finance committee will not present a budget until the Gratitude Cards have been returned. Do not give out a copy of the next year's budget or people will think we are giving to meet a church budget. Keep the focus on God's blessings in our lives. A budget will be prepared when the campaign is over, using the figures from the anticipated income from pledges as well as other sources of income to the church.

10. Invite the stewardship committee or finance committee to make phone calls the week before Gratitude Sunday to active members who have not yet made a reservation for the complementary Gratitude Brunch. Simply let the people know that we will have

a great celebration on Gratitude Sunday and need to know how many people will attend the brunch so we know how much food to prepare. Our goal is to have as many people as possible attend worship on Gratitude Sunday and participate in the process of expressing our gratitude to God.

11. On Gratitude Sunday plan an inspiring message, uplifting music, and a powerful testimony from someone about God's blessings in their lives. Have Gratitude Cards available in the bulletins or pews. After the sermon invite everyone to fill out a Gratitude Card indicating how much they plan to give each week or month during the next year to support God's work through the church. While the congregation or choir sings an appropriate song, invite people to come forward and lay their Gratitude Card on the altar or the Communion table and offer their own personal prayer of thanksgiving to God for all the blessings in their lives.

    Invite everyone to stay for the brunch whether they made reservations or not and provide food for more people than have made reservations.

    In one congregation where I was invited to preach on Gratitude Sunday there was a young couple with two children sitting near the front. The pastor realized that this was a new young family and it was their first Sunday in worship. He was concerned that we were talking about giving to God on the first Sunday they came to visit and it might turn them off from attending the church in the future. However, after the sermon this young couple filled out a Gratitude Card and came forward as a family to lay it on the altar and offer a brief prayer of thanksgiving to God. They were invited and stayed for the Gratitude Brunch.

    At the brunch the pastor visited with this new family and they explained that they had just decided to start attending church as a family and they felt blessed to be in worship on the Sunday where they got to go up to the altar and make their personal commitment to God. And they were delighted that they came on a Sunday when there was a complementary brunch and they got acquainted during a meal with others in the congregation.

    Each pastor should decide if he or she thinks it would be best if they preached on Gratitude Sunday themselves or if they should invite another pastor to preach for them on that Sunday. Sometimes pastors who know each other well swap preaching responsibilities at their friend's Gratitude Sunday service with good results.

12. Prepare the church budget for the next year on the basis of the Gratitude Cards received and other sources of church income.

    Send out a personally signed thank-you note from the pastor to everyone who has made a commitment for the next year showing the amount that was committed. People often fill out commitment cards and later can't remember how much they wrote down, so a letter with the amount pledged will be very helpful to them.

    Send out thank-you statements bi-monthly or quarterly thanking people for their giving and showing how much they committed and how much has been given to date.

    Also share stories with the congregation throughout the year of some of the wonderful ways their gifts are making a positive difference in the lives of people in their community and beyond.

Please feel free to adapt these suggestions to fit your own church or situation. My hope and prayer is that this resource will help all of us follow Christ's Generosity Path, which will lead us to revitalized generous congregations and transformed compassionate communities.

As Paul wrote to the followers of Jesus in Corinth, "We want you to excel also in this generous undertaking" (2 Cor 8:7 NRSV).

A Sample Gratitude Sunday Sermon

"Just to Say Thanks," by Kent Millard

Text: Luke 17:11-19—"One of them, when he saw that he had been healed, returned and praised God with a loud voice. He fell on his face at Jesus' feet and thanked him.... Jesus replied, 'Weren't ten cleansed? Where are the other nine?'"

Prayer: O Lord, help us to become masters of ourselves that we might be the servants of others. Take our minds and think through them, take our lips and speak through them, and take our hearts and set them on fire. Amen.

Some years ago I served for seven years as pastor at Canyon Lake United Methodist Church in Rapid City, South Dakota. Then I was appointed to serve as a district superintendent in northeastern South Dakota.

Minnietta and I had to tell our grade-school-aged children that we would be moving to a new community and I would have a new position in the church. Our son, Kendall, was in the fifth grade and when he heard the news that we were moving, he was very upset. He sat in a living room chair, folded his arms, and announced, "I'm not moving." He explained that his best friend was in Rapid City, he liked the church, and, for the first time in his life, he had a girlfriend and he was not going to leave. I explained that we were going to sell the house. He said he would rent his room from whoever bought our house but he was not going to move.

I explained that we all would be moving away from friends and that we are a family and we have to stay together. Kendall moved with us but was very unhappy about it.

The day we moved into the district parsonage, Kendall and I went downstairs to see the family room. We were surprised at what we found. There in the center of the family room was a large table with an electric train set on it all ready to run. There was also a note which read: "This train set is for Kendall. It is a gift from the Rueben Job family."

Kendall was shocked. He said, "I don't even know these people. Why would they give me such a wonderful gift?" I explained that they knew he was having a hard time moving to a new community so they wanted to do something to cheer him up.

Later, another pastor came to help us move in and brought his son who was the same age as Kendall. The boys quickly became friends and played all day with the electric train set.

The next day I was unpacking books in my home office when Kendall came into my office and plopped down a handful of coins on my desk. He said, "Dad, give this to God." I was surprised; Kendall had never done anything like that before.

I asked, "Why do you want me to give this to God?" Kendall said, "Just to say thanks." I said, "Thanks for what?" He said, "You know, John, the train, and my new bedroom."

I realized that Kendall had experienced gifts from God that he hadn't expected and he just wanted to say thanks to God for these unexpected gifts. He felt that God had been generous to him and he was grateful and he wanted to express his gratitude to God by giving God a gift.

I asked Kendall how he decided how much he was going to give to God. He said, "I opened my bank and put all the money on my bed. Then I decided to give God half of it."

I didn't tell him you only have to give 10 percent!

You see, Kendall had experienced unexpected generosity from God, his heart was filled with gratitude, and he wanted to express his gratitude by giving some of his money to God.

I believe that is the real reason any of us give some of our time, talent, and treasure to God—just to say thanks for all that God has first given us.

When we stop and think about it, we realize how generous God is to all of us. The body that we live in is a gift from God; this vehicle in which we live and move and have our being is a sheer gift from God. God gave us our mind and soul that live in this body.

The people we love—our spouses, children, grandchildren, relatives, and friends—are all a gift from the generous hand of God.

The ground we walk on, the mountains we climb, the air we breathe, the sun, the rain, the oceans and rivers, the flowers, the trees, the food we eat, the houses we live in, and this house of worship are all gifts from the hand of a generous God.

God's unconditional love for all of us that comes to us through Jesus Christ is a generous gift from the hands of our loving God.

When we stop and think about it, God has surprised all of us with God's incredible generosity to us.

Now, when someone gives one of our children a gift, as parents we often say to the child, "Now, what do you say to the one who gave you this gift?" The children then say, "Thank you."

In a similar way, we are all children of God and God has showered rich blessings on all of us and we need to remember to simply say, "Thank you, God."

Unfortunately, many of us receive all these gifts from God and simply take them for granted and fail to simply say, "Thank you."

This is what happened in the story we just read from Luke's Gospel.

Jesus and his disciples were travelling from Galilee in the north to Jerusalem in the southern part of Israel. As they approached a village, ten lepers called out to them from a distance. Now, in those days, when someone was diagnosed with the skin disease we call leprosy, they had to leave their family, their home, their work, and their village and live outside the walls of the city. It was believed that if you touched someone with leprosy, you would get it yourself, so people who had this disease that ate off parts of their body were required to live outside the village and simply beg for food from those entering and leaving the town.

So ten lepers stood at a distance and cried out to Jesus for mercy. They may have been asking for food or, if they had heard about Jesus before, asking him to heal them.

Jesus told them that they were clean, healed, and they could go back into the town and be examined by the priest to show that they were healed. As they ran back into their village, they must have marveled that their hands and faces were clean and free from this dreaded disease.

But when one of the men realized that he had been healed, he turned and went back to Jesus. He fell down on his knees and it says that he praised God with a very loud voice. He was shouting his thanksgiving to God for healing him and restoring his life. He thanked Jesus over and over for this miraculous gift of healing.

Jesus said, "Weren't ten cleansed? Where are the other nine?"

All ten were healed; all ten were generously given the gift of a new life. But only one returned to say thanks to God.

I think this is a parable of our lives today. God has given everyone the gift of life; all that we are and have is a gift from the hands of a generous God. But, frequently, we enjoy the gift but we neglect to say "thank you" to the giver.

The followers of Jesus are simply people who live with an attitude to gratitude. We come to worship simply to say "thanks" to God for all the blessings God has first given us.

One of the early church saints once said, "If the only prayer you ever said in your whole life was 'thank you,' it would be enough."

You see, we give our time, talent, and treasure to God not out of obligation or guilt, but simply to say "thank you."

Whenever we talk about stewardship and tithing, it sounds like a heavy obligation and we make people feel guilty if they don't tithe their income to God. We give to God according to our depth of gratitude to God, not because someone makes us feel guilty if we don't give.

See how much gratitude is in your heart and then decide how much of your time, talent, and treasure you will return to God.

Today we are launching our Gratitude Campaign. During the next few weeks I hope that all of us will become aware of all the gifts and blessings in our lives and, out of gratitude for these gifts, thank God by giving some of our time, talent, and treasure back to God.

Paul says that God loves a cheerful giver. I once told our congregation that the only way we can give cheerfully is if we give out of gratitude. When we count all the blessings in our lives, we want to give like Kendall did—out of gratitude just to say thanks.

I told our congregation that if they couldn't give cheerfully out of gratitude, maybe they shouldn't give at all right now. Maybe they should wait until their hearts are filled with thanksgiving and gratitude for all God has given them and then make their gift to God.

Later I met with our finance committee and they were not so happy with me. One of the men said, "We know people should give cheerfully out of gratitude, but we will still receive gifts even from a grouch."

Someone told me this little story on giving recently. A family was in church with their eight-year-old son. The offering plate was being passed around and they noticed their son had a quarter in one hand and a dime in the other. It looked like he was trying to decide which to put in the offering plate. When the plate came to him, he put in the dime.

After church his parents asked him how he decided to put in the dime rather than the quarter. The little boy said, "The preacher told us God loves a cheerful giver and I will be much more cheerful if I put in the dime."

We are often like that little boy. We often give as little as we can so we can keep more for ourselves. However, genuine joy comes when we count all the blessings God has already given us and give as much as we can just to say thanks.

My image for giving is that giving is circular. We receive gifts from God, we give back to God, and then we receive again and we give again. It is the cycle that brings meaning and joy into our lives.

This cycle is like the heart. Our heart receives blood from the rest of the body, it pumps it out again, and then it receives it again. Life requires that the blood keep flowing to keep us alive.

If the heart received blood from the rest of the body and said, "I'm going to keep it all for myself," we would die. The blood that represents life has to keep flowing to give us life.

In a similar way, we all receive the gift of life from God and we share our lives with others and then life returns to us and we share it again. This is the cycle of life. If we receive gifts from God and refuse to share them or just hold them for ourselves, we die spiritually.

I will have to confess that I did not grow up being thankful and generous. When I was little, my family never went to church because of my dad's drinking problem. So I never thought about thanking God for the blessings in my life and giving back to God out of gratitude.

Then I got married to Minnietta just before we graduated from college and she taught me to count my blessings and give generously to God. We went to seminary together at Boston University. We both had modest-paying jobs working part time in congregations and had barely enough to make ends meet. We could not afford a car, so we took public transportation everywhere we went. Our big treat was to get an ice cream cone once a week.

However, Minnietta pointed out that we did have some income so we should give a tithe or 10 percent of our modest income to God. I argued against it. I said that we barely had enough to live on so we couldn't afford to tithe and I was sure God would understand. But Minnietta persisted to putting a tithe of our income in the offering every week.

Then, I came up with what I thought was the best argument against tithing I could think of. I told her that we would be giving 100 percent of our time in serving God so we didn't have to give 10 percent of our money as well. But she didn't buy my argument and continued to put a tithe of our modest income in the offering every week.

I was focusing on what we didn't have, and she was focusing on what we did have and giving 10 percent to God out of gratitude for all the blessings in our lives.

We tithed in spite of my resistance and I was amazed that we still had enough for all of our necessities.

Then in December an amazing thing happened. We received a gift from a farmer in South Dakota that we barely knew. He sent a check for five hundred dollars, and that would be like a gift for twenty-five hundred dollars today. We were overwhelmed. He explained that each fall after he harvested his crops, he gave a tithe to God. Part of his tithe was to send a gift to a seminary student from South Dakota. He chose our name out of a list of students and sent us the gift.

His gift helped us pay our bills for months. Now, Minnietta didn't tithe because she thought we would get something in return. She tithed because she was so grateful that God had given us to each other to love and we could share God's love with others through the congregations we served. She pointed out how fortunate we were to have a little income and we should just express our gratitude to God by tithing it.

You see, I was counting how little we had to justify giving less to God. She was counting how blessed we were and wanting to be generous in expressing our gratitude to God.

It all depends on what we count. If we just count our problems, we will feel less generous. If we count our blessings, we will feel much more generous.

Our Gratitude theme this year is "Count Your Many Blessings." During the next few weeks, count your many blessings and out of gratitude for all God has given us, decide how much of your time, talent, and treasure you want to return to God during the next year.

God has blessed us all and we are full to overflowing with blessings. May we all count our many blessings, name them one by one, count our many blessings and see what God has already done in our lives. Then, out of a deep heart of gratitude, we will joyfully give some of our time, talent, and treasure back to God, "just to say thanks."

Let us pray.

Sample Gratitude Card

Front of card:

GRATITUDE CARD

You will be made rich in every way so that you can be generous in every way.
—2 Corinthians 9:11

I/We want to express my/our gratitude to God for all the blessings God has given us by giving
$_____ per ___week____month_____year
[check box] to support God's work through our church.

Print name _____
Address _____
Email _____
Signature _____
Date _____

Count your many blessings, name them one by one, count your many blessings, see what God has done.
—Johnson Oatman Jr., "Count Your Blessings"

Back of card:

THANK YOU!
Thank you for your commitment to support God's work through our congregation.

[Jesus said:] "Give, and it will be given to you. A good measure, pressed down, shaken together, running over, will be put into your lap."
—Luke 6:38 NRSV

NOTES

Introduction

1. John L. Ronsvalle and Sylvia Ronsvalle, *The State of Church Giving through 2011* (Champaign, IL: Empty Tomb, 2013), 40.

1. "Just to Say Thanks"

1. Marcus Borg, *Meeting Jesus Again for the First Time: The Historical Jesus and the Heart of Contemporary Faith* (New York: HarperCollins, 1995) 35–36.

2. Henry Smith, "Give Thanks," Integrity's Hosanna! Music, 1978.

2. Give Thanks in Every Situation

1. "Pues Si Vivimos (When We Are Living)," *The United Methodist Hymnal* (Nashville: The United Methodist Publishing House, 1989), 356. Trans. © 1989 The United Methodist Publishing House.

2. Quoted in Robert J. Furey, *The Joy of Kindness* (Crossroad, 1993), 138.

3. "Now Thank We All Our God," *The United Methodist Hymnal* (Nashville: The United Methodist Publishing House, 1989), 102.

3. Give and It Will Be Given to You

1. Roberts Emmons, "Gratitude and Well-Being," *Emmons Lab*, http://emmons.faculty.ucdavis.edu/gratitude-and-well-being/.

2. Thomas Ken, "Praise God, from Whom All Blessings Flow," *The United Methodist Hymnal* (Nashville: The United Methodist Publishing House, 1989), 95.

4. God Loves a Cheerful Giver

1. African American spiritual, "I've Got Peace Like a River," *The Faith We Sing* (Nashville: Abingdon Press, 2000), 2145.

2. Norman Cousins, *Anatomy of an Illness: As Perceived by the Patient* (New York: W.W. Norton and Company 1979), 56.

3. "O Love That Wilt Not Let Me Go," *The United Methodist Hymnal* (Nashville: The United Methodist Publishing House, 1989), 480.

4. "Joy to the World," *The United Methodist Hymnal* (Nashville: The United Methodist Publishing House, 1989), 246.

5. Expect a Miracle

1. "Miracle," *Oxford Dictionaries*, accessed March 20, 2015, http://www.oxforddictionaries.com/us/definition/american_english/miracle.

2. Lyle Schaller, "Planning and Leading a Miracle Sunday Campaign," *The Parish Paper* (August 1984).

3. Ibid.

4. Wayne C. Barrett, *The Church Finance Idea Book* (Nashville: Discipleship Resources, 1989), 96–8.

5. Larry Dossey, *Healing Words: The Power of Prayer and the Practice of Medicine* (New York: HarperCollins, 1993), xv.

6. Ibid., 179–181.

7. Randolph C. Byrd, "Positive Therapeutic Effects of Intercessory Prayer in a Coronary Care Unit Population," *Southern Medical Journal* 81:7 (July 1988), 826–29.

8. Dossey, *Healing Words*, xix.

CPSIA information can be obtained at www.ICGtesting.com
Printed in the USA
LVOW04s2026261015

459773LV00001B/1/P